BILLY GRAHAM

BILLY GRAHAM

A TRIBUTE FROM FRIENDS

Compiled by Vernon McLellan

WARNER BOOKS

An AOL Time Warner Company

Published in association with
the literary agency of Alive Communications, Inc.,
7680 Goddard Street #200, Colorado Springs, CO 80920.

 An AOL Time Warner Company

A Time Warner Company

LIBRARY OF CONGRESS CATALOGING-IN-PUBLICATION DATA

Billy Graham : a tribute from friends / Vernon McLellan.
p. cm.
ISBN 0-446-52909-5
1. Graham, Billy, 1918- I. McLellan, Vernon K.

BV3785.G69 B49 2001
269'.0'092--dc21   2001055937

Book design by Fearn Cutler de Vicq

Printed in the United States of America

First Warner Books printing: May 2002

10 9 8 7 6 5 4 3 2 1

CONTENTS

INTRODUCTION

It was my first staff meeting with *Youth for Christ International Magazine* (later to become *Campus Life*). I'd been invited to become the managing editor, following the illustrious Mel Larson. Several mature youth leaders were there. To be honest, I was scared—so young alongside these veterans! After president and publisher Ted Engstrom introduced me to everyone, he passed me a telegram. I tore it open excitedly and read these kind words: "Congratulations on being named editor of The Magazine. Be assured of my prayers. Billy Graham." I was overwhelmed and grateful (though flabbergasted). Suddenly I felt I belonged.

Several years later I was asked to become director of church relations of the Lausanne Committee for World Evangelization, which Dr. Graham founded in 1974 in Switzerland. Ever since then I have followed Dr. Graham's ministry throughout the world with enthusiasm and gratitude.

Dr. Billy Graham is not only a powerful preaching patriarch, he's a friend to many in all walks of life. For more than fifty years, this humble giant has preached the simple, unchanging gospel in a candid and compassionate manner. His spiritual wisdom and counsel have influenced many in numerous countries.

Since 1947 he has led 410 crusades involving tens of thousands of churches. This man among men—who was recently knighted by Queen Elizabeth II—has convened countless worldwide conferences and conventions that have inspired, trained, and motivated more than 125,000 pastors and evangelists to preach the gospel everywhere. He has privately prayed and counseled United States presidents, from Harry S. Truman to the present. Senators, congressmen, governors, international political leaders of differing faiths, pastors and ministry heads, business and media leaders, entertainers, sportsmen, and scores of others have all been influenced by him throughout the years.

A representative group of these men and women have paid tribute in this book to this honored and respected man.

"In times like this," Dr. Graham said at the prayer service called by President George W. Bush at the Washington National Cathedral on Friday, September 15, 2001, "we realize how weak and inadequate we are. Our greatest need is to turn in repentance and faith to the God of all mercy and the Father of all comfort. If ever there was a time for us to turn to God and to pray as a nation, it is now." Now, as always, Dr. Graham has continued to share comfort, peace, courage, and hope with millions.

What a privilege it has been to compile this book that honors one of the world's outstanding ministers. I hope you will be as inspired by these timely, heartfelt tributes as I have been.

—Vernon McLellan

BILLY GRAHAM

Dr. Ben Armstrong

Billy Graham is a role model. For me he first established this at the Christian and Missionary Alliance Council in May 1945 in Cleveland, Ohio, at Euclid Baptist Church. Billy and our mutual friend, Howard Jones, met for lunch.

Billy talked about his vision to reach the lost by preaching the gospel worldwide. It was a vision I have never forgotten. Not only did Billy have a vision for worldwide evangelism according to biblical mandates but he displayed "fire in the belly" for reaching people regardless of color or background.

Billy talked about his radio program *Songs in the Night*. That inspired me toward my own subsequent ministry in radio.

Later Billy Graham initiated his *Hour of Decision* with the help of Walter Bennett in Chicago and Fred Dienert of Philadelphia.

The result: Howard Jones joined Billy as an associate evangelist with earth-shaking achievements. Howard went to Liberia as a missionary and around the world with crusades and radio.

I was moved to tears by Billy Graham's vision of world evangelization in May 1945. It changed the course of my life. In a sense I became "radio active" for the Lord.

Dr. Ben Armstrong, Ruth Carter Stapleton, and Billy Graham
(photo courtesy of Dr. Ben Armstrong)

I helped my brother-in-law, Paul Freed, to found an international radio ministry I named Trans World Radio. For many years I labored as a TWR radio missionary in New Jersey and in Monte Carlo, Monaco.

In 1967 I founded the first national office of National Religious Broadcasters in my home basement in Madison, N.J. Sometimes discouraged during twenty-three years as executive director at National Religious Broadcasters, I never forgot Billy Graham's vision of reaching lost people. Daily prayers renewed the vision again and again.

In 1974 I was asked by Billy Graham to lead the radio/TV office of the International Congress of World Evangelization in Lausanne, Switzerland. During the meetings attended by global leaders I moderated the news conferences featuring Dr. Graham. Billy dealt courageously with strategic world issues and was always steadfastly true to the gospel as the revealed Word of God.

During the Lausanne Congress I asked Billy: "What is your key to success in evangelism?" He said: "I am greatly helped in reaching the audience by radio and TV. But every time I speak I have three objectives: (1) gain attention by dealing with the great issues of the day; (2) focus on the gospel, expressing it as clearly as I can; and (3) think about it, but always ask for a decision.

As I quote in my book *The Electric Church* (Thomas Nelson, 1979) Billy discussed his key to success in the Los Angeles Crusade in 1949. Billy said: "The crowds are larger, the interest is deeper and the response is greater. I attribute this to the power of the Holy Spirit and also to the broadcasting media open to us. . . . A great factor in the religious resurgence in this country is religious radio and television."

As executive director of National Religious Broadcasters I invited top speakers from religion and government. The most popular and frequent convention speaker was Billy Graham, keynoter from 1968 to 1989. He brought the BGEA team, including song director Cliff Barrows, soloist Beverly Shea, Howard Jones, and musicians.

At NRB you could hear Billy Graham and also a speech from the U.S. president, President Ford to President Bush.

To have Billy Graham and the president of the United States speak at NRB each year meant that religious broadcasters whatever their persuasion—fundamentalist, pentecostal, mainline, conservative, Catholic, or Protestant—attended. Mitchell includes a photo in his book *Billy Graham, Saint or Sinner* (Revell, 1979). This photo shows Billy at the NRB podium at NRB '78 with Bishop Fulton Sheen, the famous Catholic TV personality, behind him. Before the 1978 convention Bishop Sheen phoned asking me if he could attend to hear Dr. Billy Graham. Immediately I invited him to the closing banquet. After Dr. Graham's message the bishop leaned over and said to me, "What a powerful message!"

Ben Armstrong is vice president of Norstar, America's first commercial Ka-Band satellite. Before that he serves as president of Madison Broadcasting Group, Inc., and earlier as executive director of National Religious Broadcasters. He authored The Electric Church.

Wally Armstrong

My alcoholic father's coming to Jesus Christ was the greatest miracle of my life. For years he was abusive and critical of my mother and me about following Jesus.

After major cancer surgery he began reading the Bible. We saw a change in his life. He called me aside one day prior to facing more surgery, and said, "Son, a few weeks ago I took your mother down to the arena to attend a Billy Graham crusade. Dr. Graham spoke about God's love for me. He said when God forgives you He not only takes the slate of all your sins and erases it, but He takes the slate and throws it away, forever. This was the kind of forgiveness I needed. After hearing that, I took your mother's hand and we went forward and I committed my life to Jesus Christ. You do not have to worry about me. I know where I'm going."

Before Dad passed away from cancer a few months later, the last words I heard from him were those from a simple song he sang that he probably learned as a little child: "Jesus loves me! This I know, for the Bible tells me so. Little ones to Him belong. They are weak but He is strong." I wept and joy filled my soul knowing that I would see him again someday.

I am so grateful that God has so richly given Billy Graham to the world, and for the role that Billy played in being part of the greatest miracle of my life.

Wally Armstrong, president of Gator Golf Enterprises, Inc., has been a professional golfer and instructor since 1968, having competed in more than three hundred PGA Tour events. He set a rookie record in his first Masters. Because of his exceptionally consistent record, Mr. Armstrong was awarded a lifetime membership in the PGA Tour.

Kay Arthur

I have never attended a Billy Graham Crusade in person—in fact when I came to Jesus Christ at the age of twenty-nine in 1963 I really had never heard of Billy Graham, as strange as that may sound. I've only watched the BG crusades on television about two or three times. Billy and I have never personally talked more than about three times and that was never in great depth. Yet the fruit of this man's life, the spiritual by-products of the Billy Graham Association, the friendship of his various staff members, his wife, daughters, and grandchildren, and getting to know Franklin and his wife while at the Cove have all imprinted my life and my ministry.

When I reflect on Billy's impact (and it has been an impact!) on my life, I realize that it's not because of knowing him personally but of benefiting from the sum total of the way God has used him, which to me is a far greater tribute to this dear man's life.

As the cofounder of Precept Ministries International with my husband, Jack, I have learned so much about:

1. *Relationships*—maintaining long-term staff who know

Billy Graham, Kay Arthur, and Ruth Graham
(photo courtesy of Kay Arthur)

you for who you are and respect you but who are honest and objective, with no "stars in their eyes."

2. *Integrity*—in finances, in personal guidelines that help keep one beyond reproach more. How I appreciate Billy's honesty and the admonition that accompanies it.

3. *Openness*—Ruth's vulnerability, her sharing her struggles in her family, and the writing of her book about Franklin, the prodigal, all ministered to me before our own prodigal returned home.

4. *Graciousness*—the importance of the individual. When I first talked with Billy, I felt like he should be talking with others more important than me. But he never made me feel that way. There is a graciousness about Ruth and Billy that is winsome and that causes you to want to be and do the same.

I've had the privilege of partnership with the BGEA: books that I authored were offered by them, I teach at the Cove (and it's like home), I've written for *Decision Magazine,* and I serve on an advisory board for the Billy Graham Center for Evangelism. What does this say—what is the message? The message is that Billy never intended to be the star but rather one member of the body operating in his gifts and working with others in the body for the glory of the One to whom all glory belongs.

As I stand in the halls at the Cove and study the exciting pictures of Billy's beginnings as an evangelist, it's like reading Hebrews 11—my heart is stirred to press on towards the prize of the high calling in Jesus Christ. Billy is one of my heroes of faith.

Kay Arthur, along with her husband, Jack, is the founder of Precept Ministries International, a group that conducts conferences and funds institutes to train people in the Word of God. Today it serves in 118 countries in over sixty-three languages. Mrs. Arthur has written over forty books including How to Study Your Bible.

Dr. David Breese

Billy Graham has had a profound influence upon my life. We first met in my last year of seminary and quickly developed a warm friendship. It was obvious to everyone that Billy was going to be an evangelist! I was torn between a love of teaching and a burning desire to reach a world for Christ. Billy's zeal and fire for the Lord helped lead me to my decision. I would teach, but I would do it from the podium of the evangelist.

In the years that followed, we worked together on several occasions. It was my privilege to speak to the youth at the Minneapolis crusade, which drew thousands. During the years in which "Youth for Christ" exploded across the world, we met abroad many times at the annual YFC World Congresses. The interaction with Christians from other lands produced in us a heightened passion for evangelism.

Billy Graham and I have fought together as soldiers on a battlefield for the Lord. I respect him as a warrior of the cross and a defender of the gospel. His ability to explain the gospel simply and clearly is without peer. He is a faithful servant of the Almighty God, and it warms my soul to be able to call him my friend.

Dr. David Breese is an internationally known author, lecturer, broadcaster, and minister. He is president of Christian Destiny, Inc., and World Prophetic Ministry. Dr. Breese is the author of several books including Seven Men Who Rule the World from the Grave.

Dr. Bill Bright

Billy Graham has been a great inspiration to me for over a half century. No one has had a greater impact on world evangelism and on more people, nor has maintained such a total focus on the gospel of our Lord Jesus Christ than has Billy.

In 1951 God called my wife, Vonette, and me to begin the worldwide ministry of Campus Crusade for Christ International, just three years after Billy came on the national scene. The last half of the twentieth century and continuing has been an incredible, unprecedented time of harvest for God's kingdom, with other great worldwide ministries also established during this time. There has never been such a time in the history of the church, largely because of the explosion of technology and transportation. I believe God anointed Billy Graham to help spearhead this great move of the Holy Spirit.

Many years ago, while I was a student at Fuller Theological Seminary and running my own business, two very gifted young evangelists came to speak during a chapel program. Both believed and preached the Word of God without questioning its authority. Later, however, both began to question whether or not the Bible was truly inspired in every way and in every

Bill Bright, Billy Graham, and Vonette Bright
(photo courtesy of Bill Bright)

word. One of these men eventually rejected the integrity of God's Word. As a result, he had no moorings on which to base his life and ministry. He got a divorce, left the ministry, and eventually became an outspoken antagonist of the Christian faith.

The other young man chose to believe that the Bible was truly the Word of God. Even what he could not understand, he entrusted to God and reckoned it to be true, until such time as God would grant understanding.

There is no need for me to mention the name of the first man. But the second man is my good friend Billy Graham. I have always admired Billy's faithfulness to God's holy, inerrant Word.

During a sermon by Billy I was once inspired to take on a task that would be impossible without God's intervention. It was in about 1969, and I was at a Billy Graham evangelistic crusade in Minneapolis. Billy was speaking. As he spoke, another voice began speaking to my heart, telling me to call a great gathering of one hundred thousand people together for a week of training in discipleship and evangelism.

It was clearly God speaking to me. I was so excited I could hardly contain myself. I later shared the idea with Billy and he became excited, saying, "I want to help."

The idea would be an enormous undertaking. Not all of our ministry leadership was enthusiastic about the idea. Some doubted. I could have been discouraged, but was determined to obey God. And by His grace, following much planning and hard work, it finally came about. Explo '72 was the greatest event of its kind in history, resulting in eighty-five thousand people coming for a week of training in the Spirit filled life and evangelism. On the final day, some two hundred thousand came for praise and worship led by Billy Graham, Johnny Cash, and other famous musicians. Billy was used by God to inspire me for this project, then God used him to help in the program.

Through the years Billy has been involved in many of our various projects and I have been privileged to participate in all of his world conferences on evangelism and other events.

I thank God for Billy Graham, my friend, my brother, and my fellow servant in Christ.

Bill Bright, along with his wife, Vonette, founded Campus Crusade for Christ International in 1951. Since then CCCI has grown into an organization that includes sixty ministries in 186 countries. Dr. Bright has written more than fifty books including Four Spiritual Laws.

Vonette Zachary Bright

Friendship with the Grahams began with a luncheon at the Tick-Tock Restaurant in Hollywood with Henrietta Mears, Billy Graham, and ourselves in early 1949. Bill and I had been married only a few weeks. I remember being favorably impressed with Billy's enthusiasm for Christ and his delightful personality. As the years developed, our lives became intertwined in various ways.

One of the most fulfilling and rewarding experiences of my life developed as a result of Dr. Graham's invitation for me to be one of three women in the fifty original members of the Lausanne Committee for World Evangelization. Concerned about the problems facing our culture in the sixties and seventies, I began to explore and speak about what women might do to counteract or inspire solution to the counter cultured movement. I shared my concern with Ruth Graham and three others on what action might be taken. Ruth Graham shared how she felt the answer was to mobilize women to pray. We agreed and launched The Great Commission Prayer Crusade, a movement to unite Christians to pray strategically and specifically for local, national, and international needs. Ruth Graham and I spoke to seven thousand women in the Los Angeles Sports Arena for our first event, which helped the ministry become a catalyst in helping Christians worldwide unite in prayer.

The invitation to become a member of the Lausanne Committee and the assignment to the intercession advisor group allowed me to promote worldwide the dream God had placed in my heart for the United States. Billy Graham was very complimentary of my efforts and his expressed confidence, along with my husband's encouragement, gave me the courage to attempt goals that I had never previously dreamed of being able to accomplish. It was Dr. Graham who gave the first large gift for The International Prayer Assembly, which I chaired, in Seoul, Korea. The LCWE and the Korean Evangelical Fellowship sponsored this event and it was the largest international meeting for prayer ever held at the time.

There are many events that have been held in association with the Grahams that stand out as highlights. The 1949 crusade in Los Angeles, The Hollywood Bowl Crusade, was where as a counselor I first learned to share my faith. That experience prepared me to be all the more receptive to the concept of Campus Crusade for Christ when the Lord revealed it to my husband. Within the first year of the ministry, Billy Graham gave the largest check that had been given at that time—one thousand dollars. His contribution was a tremendous encouragement.

We have been privileged to attend each of the Congresses of Evangelism, the first in Berlin in 1966 and the last in

Amsterdam 2000, where Bill and I were asked to speak depicting fifty years of marriage and ministry. It has been a great pleasure to see the friendship and camaraderie grow and be maintained between my husband and Billy Graham. They have supported each other's ministry through the years and have been available to speak for each other when needed.

One of the most memorable and hilarious experiences that we recall was during Dr. Graham's first campaign in Los Angeles. My husband and I invited Billy Graham to dinner. Ruth was not in Los Angeles at that time. When Billy Graham accepted, we were excited about entertaining him and naïve about what that meant. At that time our home was a small two-bedroom English cottage, a former guest house to a larger home. We had anticipated serving a small party, including Billy and an assistant or two. As newlyweds, we had only a few sets of china and I insisted we purchase something matching. We chose pottery from a Franciscan China Outlet that were gigantic-sized plates requiring an enormous amount of food to fill—a mistake I had to live with for a long time.

I stayed home that night to finish preparing the meal while Bill attended the service. When he returned, he brought Billy's entire team, including Cliff Barrows, Grady and T. W. Wilson, George Beverly Shea, Susie and Stewart Hamlin, and others. Stewart was a Western entertainer in Hollywood and not yet a Christian. He was a master at telling tall-tales, but so were Grady and T. W., who really kept us in stitches all evening.

Stewart could not have helped being impressed that Christians really do have more fun. Shortly after, he made a commitment to Christ. Susie realized my food-shortage predicament and pitched in to help me prepare more food. Where it all came from I'll never know! But we had plenty to eat.

I realized later how shocked the team must have been at our modest arrangements after being entertained in some of the most prominent homes of Los Angeles. No one said a word. Now, as we come across those whom we met that night, we nearly always mention the fun of that evening.

Billy and Ruth Graham have made a profound impact upon the world. We are so grateful their lives have touched ours. I am particularly grateful for the encouragement and support that both of them have been to me. I cherish our friendship and delight in every memory of which they are a part.

Vonette Zachary Bright is co-founder of Campus Crusade for Christ. She also founded the Great Commission Prayer Crusade, the National Prayer Committee, and Women Today International, as well as work toward legislation for the National Day of Prayer held each May. As part of the Lausanne Committee for World Evangelization in 1974, she served as chairwoman of the International Prayer Assembly for World Evangelism in Korea. She is the author of several books including For Such a Time as This.

George H. W. Bush

We Bushes have so many wonderful memories and thoughts about Billy Graham. We have admired him from afar, watching him deliver his powerful message during his many crusades. We have sat mesmerized in churches as he led us and the entire nation in prayer. He has spoken in our two little churches in Maine, teaching the sermons about Jesus Christ our Savior just as if he was preaching to one hundred thousand people in a major crusade somewhere here or abroad.

And we have seen him in our home, in the bosom of our family, talking to our grandkids about the real meaning of life and about Jesus. And heaven and sin. And wonder.

One particularly poignant moment for us was when Billy was visiting us here in Maine, which he did from time to time. My mother—whose faith was strong, whose knowledge of the Bible was great, and whose life was full of Christian love—invited Dr. Graham to walk across from our house to her little bungalow for a private breakfast. Billy had always been so kind and considerate to my beloved mother. The two of them sat quietly and read some Bible passages and Billy said a prayer. Later that day Mother said to me, "That was the most glorious time of my life." She loved the man. All Bushes do.

George H.W. Bush, Barbara Bush, and Billy Graham
(photo courtesy of George Bush Presidential Library)

The day I was sworn in as president, my ailing mother was watching the parade from the window of the Queen's Bedroom in the White House. Dr. Graham saw her and left the parade to sit next to her and keep her company.

Billy came to stay with Barbara and me at the White House on the eve of the air war against Iraq. I told him what I was now having to do, our diplomacy and our quest for a peaceful solution having failed. I told him when the first cruise missiles would hit Baghdad, and we watched in wonder as the war to liberate Kuwait began. Just the three of us were there. Billy said a little prayer for our troops and for the innocents who might be killed. The next day we attended a church service at Fort Meade. His very presence brought great comfort to the people in uniform who were praying at that special service.

I cannot begin to tell what Billy's presence and his faith meant to me as president and as commander in chief. His own beliefs and abiding faith gave me great strength.

Billy is particular close to our current president, George W. Bush. His wonderful son Franklin flew Billy to our son's inauguration as governor in Austin, Texas, back in 1994. And then when George became the forty-third president of the United States, Billy was again at his side, leading the nation in prayer as he had done for me when I took the oath of office in 1989. He has counseled the president and given him strength just as he did for me. This counsel—indeed friendship—did not begin just when George W. became president. It is a friendship that started years ago with a number of heart-to-heart talks and which has grown stronger through the years. Billy has been a true inspiration to the president.

Billy was always considerate of administrations in Washington, not wanting to cause problems by traveling to places where a visit from him might complicate our foreign policy or relations with a specific country. Once he called me about a trip to Russia he was planning to take. Did I think the trip would make things more difficult for the administration? I of course said, "No, go on your trip." He went and indeed I truly believe that visit gave hope to those in Russia who craved religious freedom. He did the same in China and Korea. His message of faith and love resonate wherever he goes.

The Bush family is indeed blessed to call this great man a friend. We love him as a brother. Our sons and daughter love him as a father. And all of us love him as a wise counselor.

After serving as the then youngest pilot in the Navy, George H.W. Bush turned to politics. In 1966 he became the first Republican to represent Houston in the House of Representatives. He followed that with a stint as chairman of the Republican National Committee before his appointment as director of the CIA. In 1979 President Bush was elected vice president under Ronald Reagan. In 1989 he was inaugurated as the forty-first president of the United States.

Robert Byrd

I have long admired Billy Graham. His strong faith in the Creator, his ability to inspire millions of people around the globe through that faith, and his manner of incorporating that faith in his everyday life are incomparable. His work has enriched the spiritual side of life for peoples around the entire world. I consider myself fortunate to have had the opportunity to meet the Reverend Dr. Graham and to tell him personally of my deep admiration for his commitment to strengthening the spiritual and moral foundation in our society.

Billy Graham's faith is genuine. His faith is strong. He does not leave God's Word at the church on Sunday. For him the Lord's work is an all day, every day, commitment. Our nation and in fact the world are richer places in spirit because of his dedicated and persevering work.

Senator Robert Byrd has represented West Virginia since 1959. In 1971 he defeated Senator Edward Kennedy for the position of Senate majority whip and later served as both minority and majority leader. From 1989 to 1995 Senator Byrd chaired the Senate appropriations committee.

Ralph Carmichael

Although we have never golfed or dined together, I consider Dr. Billy Graham one of my most treasured friends.

About fifty years ago I was driving my car down Vine Street in Hollywood with my radio set on the local ABC station. I had heard that Dr. Graham's very first national broadcast was to be aired that Sunday. I waited breathlessly through the station I.D. and then I heard Cliff Barrows announce *The Hour of Decision,* followed by the crusade choir singing, "Glory, Glory, Hallelujah." What a thrill! I wanted to roll down my window and shout to passing motorists, "Turn your radios to the ABC network!"

What a glorious day that was for Christendom everywhere! Dr. Graham gave the evangelical message a national voice and has continued faithfully in that role for a half a century.

Also, what a glorious day it was for me to be asked by producer Dick Ross to do Billy's first feature film in 1951, called *Mr. Texas.*

Do I believe in divine providence? I sure do. God put me in the right place at the right time. My years of service in the creation of film scores for Dr. Graham have been rich and ful-

Billy Graham and Ralph Carmichael
(photo courtesy of Ralph Carmichael / Carmichael Enterprises)

filling (eighteen film scores and many gospel songs, including "He's Everything To Me").

I am so happy to be able to publicly thank Dr. Graham for all he has meant to me over the last half century.

Ralph Carmichael is a music arranger, conductor, writer, producer, and record executive who has crossed the barriers of music genres. He was one of the driving forces behind the creation of "contemporary Christian music." He wrote film scores for World Wide Pictures, the company that produced full-length movies for the Billy Graham Evangelism Association. Among other songs, he is the composer of the hit "Born Free."

President Jimmy Carter, Ruth Graham, Billy Graham,
and Rosalynn Carter
(photo courtesy of Jimmy Carter Library)

Jimmy Carter

I can think of no individual in the twentieth century (and now in the start of the twenty-first) who has so positively influenced as many lives as Reverend Billy Graham. His goal of helping others find and enjoy a personal relationship with Christ has led him around the world for more than half a century. His invitation to receive Christ has been extended to and received by individuals in every walk of life. I am grateful to Dr. Graham for the generous personal counsel he gave me during my presidency and in the years since.

After graduating from the U.S. Naval Academy and serving for several years, President Carter returned to Georgia and served as both senator and governor before election to the post of the thirty-ninth president of the United States in 1976. Since finishing his term he has been busy in humanitarian efforts through Habitat for Humanity and his own organization, The Carter Center. President Carter is the author of over a dozen books including Keeping Faith: Memoirs of a President.

N o true evangelist has emphasized the Bible as strongly as Billy Graham. Actually, he has encouraged ministers around the world to preach out of the Bible. He explains the history of mankind through the Bible. He expounds on current situations using the Bible, and through the Bible he prepares people for the future. So he has really introduced the Bible to the hearts and minds of people. We praise the Lord for that.

As Koreans, we really appreciate Billy Graham because when he came to Korea he led a history-breaking evangelistic crusade at Yoido Plaza here in Seoul with one million people in attendance. Until that time we had never dreamed of seeing one million people gather together in one place. But since then, we have had many gatherings of one million people at Yoido Plaza. This is because the Billy Graham crusade inspired the Korean Church to have faith for such great rallies. Billy Graham's ministry inspired all the Korean churches and the Korean Church began to have a vision to evangelize all of Korea. Now we have about twelve million members in the Korean Church. Billy Graham contributed tremendously to this evangelization by coming to Korea several times.

As for me personally, I'm greatly indebted to his life and magnanimity because when we were celebrating one hundred years of the Korean Church, some didn't want to accept me into the celebration because I am from the Assemblies of God. But Billy Graham was invited to speak at the convocation and he strongly insisted that I should be included. So they accepted his recommendation and I was adopted as one of the speakers at the celebration. Since that time, I have a very close fellowship with all the denominations—especially Presbyterians. I have a feeling that has come about through the love and ministry of Billy Graham.

The world has been tremendously blessed through the ministry of Billy Graham. I remember when I went to Holland to attend one of his worldwide meetings and saw ministers from around the world gather together to listen and learn. I was greatly impressed because his ministry has really given life to the churches around the world. We will praise God for Dr. Billy Graham until Christ returns.

A former Buddhist, Dr. David Yonggi Cho is senior pastor of Seoul, Korea's Yoido Full Gospel Church, the largest church in the world. He is also CEO of David Cho Evangelistic Mission and founder of Church Growth International, a forum for sharing biblical principles. Dr. Cho is the author of over one hundred books including The Nature of God.

I first saw Billy Graham in person when he preached in Little Rock's War Memorial Stadium in the late 1950s, during the racial crisis that followed the closing of Little Rock Central High School. Many influential white citizens urged Billy to close the crusade to blacks, allegedly to avoid the possibility of an incident. He refused and said he would cancel the crusade before he would speak to a segregated audience. I was thrilled by his strong principled stand and by the fact that my Sunday school teacher took me and a few other grade school boys to hear him. I still remember the enormous power of blacks and whites walking down onto the football field together when Billy invited them to profess their faith in Christ.

Thirty years later I met Billy for the first time when he came back to Little Rock for another crusade. I was governor then and eager to welcome him. Billy was an old friend of my pastor, W. O. Vaught, who was desperately ill and knew he didn't have long to live.

I took Billy to see Dr. Vaught and sat quietly as the two great ministers reviewed their decades of friendship, their triumphs and struggles, and their feeling about the death that comes to us

President Bill Clinton and Billy Graham
(photo courtesy of White House Photography)

all. They talked about the Holy Land and its eternal promise. When the time came for us to go, Billy took Dr. Vaught's frail hand in his and said, "W. O., it won't be too long for both of us. I'll see you just outside the Eastern Gate." It was a moment I'll never forget. I've kept a picture of the three of us on that day in my home ever since.

When I became president, Billy counseled me and prayed with and for me as he had with so many of my predecessors.

He gave the invocation at both my inaugurals. We talked about lots of things and I was always inspired by his wise insights into world leaders and their problems. He and Ruth were always so kind and gracious to Hillary. He wrote and talked on the phone. And visited me after the pain of my private sin became public and the subject of political debate. We talked about repenting, atonement, and forgiveness. He was a source of strength, reassurance, and faith beyond my ability to relate.

Billy Graham has touched hundreds of millions of lives with the power and eloquence of his Christian commitment. He has helped many people in positions of power and influence keep or regain their bearings and live by their convictions. He is larger than life to so many. But to me, he is a friend, a model of Christian charity, an intensely human pastor. As an eleven-year-old boy, a young governor, a president, I looked to him and saw the spirit of God reaching out to all the troubled souls. I am privileged to have been one of them.

Bill Clinton served five terms as governor of Arkansas between 1978 and 1990. He was then elected forty-second president of the United States and served two terms, from 1992 to 2000. President Clinton is a graduate of Yale Law School and a Rhodes Scholar.

Daniel Coats

I was first introduced to Billy Graham nearly fifty years ago while listening to *The Hour of Decision* on the car radio while my mother was visiting an ill friend. I was moved by the music of George Beverly Shea, the strength and truth of Billy's preaching, and his invitation to come to Christ "Just as I am."

My young heart was touched by Christ that day, and He has directed my thoughts and paths ever since. God has blessed me along the way with Christian parents, a sound Baptist church upbringing, a Wheaton College education, a Christian wife and friends, and so much more.

Billy Graham introduced me to Christ nearly fifty years ago. In June 1999 I was privileged to share my faith on the closing night of the crusade in Indianapolis. I cannot adequately describe my emotions as I joined Billy, Bev Shea, and others on the platform. I watched, prayed and praised the Lord as thousands came forward to receive Christ—just like I'd done so long ago.

Daniel Coats represented the State of Indiana in the U.S. Senate from 1989 to 1999. He has served as cochair, along with Senator Joseph

Andrew Coats, Marcia Coats, Senator Dan Coats, and Billy Graham
(photo courtesy of Senator Dan Coats)

Lieberman, of the Center for Jewish and Christian Values. He has also served as president of Big Brother/Big Sisters of America. Mr. Coats currently works with former majority leaders Bob Dole and George Mitchell as special counsel with a Washington, D.C., law firm.

Twenty-seven years ago, my life was dramatically changed. In the midst of Watergate, seeing all of the things I had worked for and the president (Richard Nixon) whom I had served falling from grace, a very good friend told me one evening about Jesus Christ. I left his home that night but I was crying so hard I couldn't drive my automobile. In a flood of tears, alone in my automobile in my friend's driveway, I surrendered my life to Christ. Nothing has been the same since or ever can be again.

It turns out the man who witnessed to me, Tom Phillips, then the president of the Raytheon company, had been converted at a Billy Graham Crusade in Madison Square Garden in New York City in 1968. How unlikely are God's ways? Here was the head of one of the largest corporations in America going forward with a stream of repentant sinners and then returning to his business where four years after I left the White House, I returned to be his Washington counsel. Phillips shared his faith with me at the darkest moment in my life. And from that encounter has come my experience in prison and then the launching of a ministry that is now active in eighty-eight coun-

Billy Graham and Charles Colson
(photo courtesy of Charles Colson/Prison Fellowship)

tries, reaching into literally thousands of prisons, touching countless hundreds of thousands of lives. This is how the gospel spreads, Graham to Phillips to Colson.

So it is that I am a Billy Graham disciple one step removed, but my debt to Graham goes far beyond that. I had known Billy when he came to the White House to visit President Nixon. He was the preacher; I was the president's chief political operative. But after my conversion I came to know him in a much different way. Billy reached out to me, befriended me, guided me and counseled me. He has served as a role model, a person I could emulate as we built our ministry.

I have many rich memories of my experiences with Billy Graham, but none more meaningful than the day he and I toured the Memphis Federal Prison. He had spoken outside to one thousand inmates gathered from three separate institutions. After it was over, I asked Billy if he would go into the maximum-security segregation unit to see those men who could not come out to hear him speak. Though his aides were pulling him back to the hotel to rest up for a crusade that night in Memphis, Billy instantly agreed. We toured the cold, stark cellblock, and I watched Billy Graham—clearly the greatest evangelist of the twentieth century—as he sat on the floor talking through the grate in a cell door to lead an inmate to Christ. There was no press present, no crowds to impress. This was the real Graham, caring for the least of these and not willing to leave that prison until even the outcasts of that institution had heard the gospel.

For me, Billy Graham has not only been a spiritual mentor but a public figure who has never failed his trust. He has remained humble and God-fearing, resisting all the temptations that come with celebrity. He will be remembered for many, many things, not the least of which is his authenticity.

Charles W. Colson is chairman of the board for Prison Fellowship, launched after his release from prison in 1975 for circumstances related to Watergate. He is now considered one of America's leading authorities on the causes of and responses to crime. Mr. Colson has written more than twenty books including his bestseller Born Again.

Dr. W. A. Criswell

Back yonder in the days gone into history, Billy Graham became a young evangelist with infinite potentiality. He held crusades in the great cities of our nation and they were attended by thousands and thousands of people. In those same meaningful days, Billy Graham became a member of our First Baptist Church here in Dallas and has remained as such through the following scores of years.

It would be impossible to portray too much of all that Billy Graham has meant to our people and to the world. God be praised for the incomparable evangelistic ministry of Billy Graham.

A former president of the Southern Baptist Convention, Dr. W. A. Criswell became pastor of First Baptist Church in Dallas in 1944. Since then the church has grown to a membership totaling over twenty-eight thousand. It supports thirty-one mission chapels and owns and operates First Baptist Academy and The Criswell College, of which Dr. Criswell is chancellor. Dr. Criswell is the author of over fifty books.

Paul Crouch

Jan and I met Dr. Billy Graham for the first time in Forrest Home, California, in 1968. Billy Graham's enduring, selfless passion for souls inspired us then and continues to inspire and ignite the fire for Christian evangelism—the impetus to preach the Gospel to the whole world—today.

In 1980 TBN had the joy of carrying the Billy Graham crusade from Reno, Nevada, live via satellite. At that crusade, Dr. Graham thanked Trinity Broadcasting Network for carrying the crusade live across America and acknowledged that this new satellite technology being used to carry the gospel was indeed part of the fulfillment of the Bible prophecy recorded by John in the Book of Revelation:

> And I saw another angel fly in the midst of heaven, having the everlasting gospel to preach unto them that dwell on the earth, and to every nation, and kindred, and tongue, and people, saying with a loud voice, Fear God, and give glory to Him; for the hour of His judgment is come: and worship Him that made heaven, and earth, and the sea, and the fountains of waters. (Rev. 14:6-7 KJV)

Billy Graham, Paul Crouch, and Jan Crouch
(photo courtesy of Trinity Broadcasting Network)

TBN also covered the great Billy Graham crusade from Anaheim, California, and most recently had the honor of carrying Amsterdam 2000, the historic Billy Graham conference that inspired a new generation of evangelists from 209 nations and territories. Because of the joint effort of the Billy Graham Evangelistic Association and Trinity Broadcasting Network in televising this historic conference, not only were the lives of all the evangelists who were in attendance touched, but untold multitudes who were watching, as well, from literally around the world (via fifteen satellites!).

Jan and I, and all of the TBN family, join in expressing our appreciation of Dr. Billy Graham, who continues to preach the simple gospel of Jesus Christ and who has become the foremost ambassador, inspirational role model, and standard-bearer for Christian evangelism.

Paul Crouch began his career in radio and television in the early 1950s when he built an educational AM radio station (KCBI) on the campus of Central Bible Institute and Seminary. In 1973 Paul and Jan founded the Trinity Broadcasting Network, Inc., a nonprofit corporation based in California that broadcasts Christian programs around the world. Along with his wife, Jan, Dr. Crouch and TBN have been recipients of numerous awards and citations.

I t is extremely difficult for me to put into proper perspective what a great servant of God Billy Graham is. I will tell
you of two experiences I had that have made a great impression
on me.

Having been raised in the church (as I am a minister's
daughter), the words integrity, honesty, and consistency were
very important to me. I saw my father represent all of those
attributes to me, yet I could point to dozens in the church who
couldn't. I am grateful for the few who did, otherwise I'm sure
I would not be a Christian today, because I was very angry at
the church for their failure to represent to me those qualities.

To become associated in friendship as well as in ministry
with Billy and Ruth Graham was a wonderful experience for
me. Billy, Ruth, Fred (my husband) and I were once together for
a convention. I turned to Bill and asked, "If I wanted to give you
a personal check to be used for a project you and Ruth have
planned for your home or for yourselves, would you take it?"

He said, "No, I would not."

"Now, wait a minute," I said. "Why wouldn't you want to
fulfill an honest desire your friends have for your benefit?"

He replied, "Millie, I made a commitment to the Lord when I went into full-time ministry that I would always operate on the salary determined for me or income from an outside project that I worked on, such as my books. I would take no extra gifts or income from an individual nor anything personal from an individual."

"That isn't fair," I said.

"It may not be fair to you but it is fair to the world who is waiting and watching for anyone visible in God's family to take gifts for themselves. I want to honor the Lord at all times, thereby turning over to the Billy Graham Evangelistic Association every gift that is given to me personally. And I will do so until I die."

That situation spoke volumes to me. I realized that his commitment to the Lord on personal financial matters was far greater than his own personal desires for himself.

In a totally different venue, the other incident was when we were celebrating Ruth's birthday in a little restaurant in the mountains. Both Fred and Bill had known the owner of this restaurant for many years. My husband called the owner on the phone and told him of Ruth's upcoming birthday and asked if he would prepare a special meal (as he was also an excellent gourmet cook) and perhaps invite a few local people to come in to serenade us with Ruth's favorite songs. The owner went "all out" to do everything Fred had asked him to do because of the impact Dr. Graham had had on his spiritual life. That, in itself, left an impression on me. When a restaurateur is impacted by a man's life and attitude away from the platform, that indicates real consistency.

This restaurateur wanted to make an evening of special music and fun as well. So he rented a curly, long-haired red wig for Ruth to wear. Well, Ruth did, and it was hilarious. In between courses, he came up behind Ruth, took off the wig and put it on Bill's head. For one long minute, Bill sat there spellbound, with a look of shock on his face. While we were all howling with laughter, Bill finally joined us, saying, "Maybe I need to keep this on since you are all enjoying my appearance so much."

I saw, once again, someone who could enjoy and be part of the fun times of life. He has actually referred to that particular incident frequently with fondness. Fred and I became aware of Bill's sensitivity to the need for celebration of life as well as the celebration of his relationship with God.

Every time I look at the pictures I am reminded of how great a servant of God he truly is, because he agrees with Paul: "I can be all things to all men." I have found that to be very true. I'm glad the Lord gave us muscles in our faces to smile and to laugh and not just to shed the tears in our eyes.

Millie Dienert began teaching small Bible classes in her home almost five decades ago. Since then she has come to be known as the First Lady of Prayer for her continued intercessory work for people around the world. She was named American Churchwoman of the Year in 1990 by Religious Heritage of America. Most recently Mrs. Dienert was appointed "prayer chair" for Amsterdam 2000, a conference of preaching evangelists.

Dr. James C. Dobson

N̲o one has made a greater impact on today's world for the sake of Christ than Dr. Billy Graham. He has faithfully preached the Word to literally millions of people over the years, taking the Good News to lost and hurting souls all over the globe. He has demonstrated the love of Jesus to the powerful and influential leaders of nations as well as to the poor and downtrodden masses in the slums and townships of the Third World. Through it all, Billy Graham's humility and servant-like attitude have remained a constant, as he has avoided the pursuit of fame and recognition in favor of answering Christ's call to "make disciples of all nations."

Shirley and I first met Billy Graham in 1983 when we were asked to participate in his Calgary crusade. I was sitting on the platform when he came over to introduce himself. I stood and shook his hand, saying, "I'm so glad to meet you, Dr. Graham." He smiled and immediately said, "Okay, don't call me that—call me Billy." Frankly, I found it very difficult to comply with his request because of my profound respect for him.

Billy Graham has represented the cause of Christ for all these years, and his name has never been associated with scandal or moral failure. I admire him for keeping his eyes fixed on the prize and for diligently walking the straight-and-narrow.

Dr. James C. Dobson is founder and president of Focus on the Family, and a licensed psychologist and marriage, family, and child counselor. Dr. Dobson's first book, Dare to Discipline, *has now sold over three million copies and was selected as one of fifty books to be placed in the White House Library.*

Dr. Ted Engstrom

I first met Billy Graham in the fall of 1947, shortly after he graduated from Wheaton College. I was in the book publishing business at that time as editor at Zondervan Publishing House and as a volunteer was directing the ministry of Youth for Christ in Grand Rapids, Michigan. We decided to sponsor a youth crusade in the city and heard about this young evangelist who was so gifted. I invited Billy to come be our evangelist and he conducted what became his first citywide crusade in the year 1947. We thought it was a large meeting at the time, filling the 5,500 seat Civic Auditorium in the city, but it was just a forerunner of his magnificent crusades in the following decades.

Since that first contact with Billy, he has become a close friend and I've met with him on numerous occasions.

At one time he invited me to meet with him in his mother's home in Charlotte and indicated his interest in beginning a magazine as part of his ministry. This later became *Decision Magazine,* published by the Billy Graham Evangelistic Association. At that time, Billy asked if I would be willing to come with him to serve as editor of the publication. I did not feel the

Dr. Ted Engstrom and Billy Graham
(photo courtesy of Dr. Ted Engstrom)

leading of the Lord to do this but was complimented by his offer.

On another occasion, a decade or so ago, he called me and said he was going to be in San Francisco for a free day and wondered if I could come up and spend a day with him. I told him I would drop everything in order to spend such choice time together. I met him at a hotel near the airport and we spent the entire day together simply chatting and fellowshiping. He primarily wanted to talk about mutual friends and what was happening in these various arenas in which we both had keen interest. It was an unforgettable day to spend the time alone with him for those eight or nine hours.

There is no individual I admire or appreciate more than my beloved friend Billy. His marvelous modesty is most becoming; he's indeed God's chosen servant for this generation. When he moves on to be with the Lord he will be tremendously missed and there will be a vacuum in our evangelical leadership.

I salute this choice friend as the most significant leader of our generation.

Former president and chief executive officer of World Vision and now president emeritus, Ted Engstrom is one of the most influential leaders in American religion and social services. He has also served as president of Youth for Christ International and Azusa Pacific University. Dr. Engstrom has written over fifty books, including the bestseller The Making of a Christian Leader.

Dr. Anthony Evans

D r. Billy Graham holds a special place in my heart for a number of very special reasons. First, his unwillingness to participate in segregated crusades during a time in our history when the racial divide was at its worst testifies to his authenticity. He established a standard of racial unity and harmony that most of evangelicalism at the time had rejected. This act of godliness that addressed one of the most graphic evils to plague the nation and the church showed Dr. Graham to be a biblicist in the social arena. It showed he not only recognized that the souls of all men were equally in need of the gospel, but also that bodies in which these souls were housed needed to be equally respected. He rejected the criticism of his Christian contemporaries and not only endured the wrath but took the additional step of hiring black evangelists, thus integrating his ministry in a time of segregation. His consistent position in this regard is one of the great legacies of his ministry, and one for which I will be eternally grateful.

On a personal note, I am grateful for the encouragement he has given to me and my family. I will never forget the day I was speaking at the Cove in Asheville, North Carolina, and I re-

Dr. Tony Evans, a friend, and Billy Graham
(photo courtesy of Dr. Tony Evans)

ceived word that Dr. and Mrs. Graham wanted to have dinner
with me and hear me speak that evening. His words of encouragement of how my radio broadcast had encouraged him and
how vital my ministry was to the body of Christ was what I
needed from God that day. The Lord used our time together to
let me know in a special way that He was indeed using me.

On another occasion I was invited up to his home for a

time of fellowship. On this occasion he let me know that he prayed for me. The fact that I was on his spiritual radar screen given all the people and ministries that he has a much greater contact with was especially energizing.

Finally, my son Anthony Jr., who went to Liberty University with Dr. Graham's grandsons, was invited to have Thanksgiving dinner with the Graham family. He shared with me how kind, humble, and encouraging Dr. Graham was to him during the visit. It meant a great deal to both me and my son to know that the man revered by millions was as sincere in private as he is in public.

Only eternity will manifest all Dr. Billy Graham has meant to the Kingdom of God. I am thankful that I have had the privilege of having him and his wife, Ruth, not only as giants of faith but also as personal friends.

Dr. Anthony Evans is senior pastor of the Oak Cliff Bible Fellowship in Dallas. He is also founder and president of The Urban Alternative, a national organization seeking to bring about spiritual renewal in urban America. The Alternative with Dr. Tony Evans *is heard on over five hundred radio stations around the country. Dr. Evans is author of several books including* Free at Last.

F or many, many years, I have listened to and seen some of Dr. Billy Graham's programs on radio and television. I admire his ability to cooperate with the enlightenment of the Holy Spirit and with the power of the Holy Spirit to make the scriptures relevant to everyone. He responds in one way or another to the needs of all people who are definitely searching for the empowerment of the Holy Bible, the Word of God, and the promptings of the Holy Spirit. Reverend Billy Graham has been concerned with helping and directing people . . . he has never been concerned about opposing or attacking people. He has been very respectful of those who perhaps have different convictions but nonetheless are trying to find and follow the Lord.

In all the times that I have listened to Dr. Graham's programs, never once have I heard him attack our church or other churches that have different approaches or different points of view. He simply makes the presentation of the Scriptures applicable to each and every one of us in a very good and healthy way.

When the pope was coming to San Antonio in 1987, Dr. Graham encouraged all the non-Catholics of the area to try to be present, to welcome the pope, and to listen to his messages. I was very grateful to him for this great and wonderful support. When Dr. Graham came to San Antonio the last time, I encouraged Catholics to participate at his general presentations or wherever it was possible because I was sure that those who attended and listened to his talks would definitely be inspired and guided by his messages . . . and that was truly the case.

Dr. Billy Graham could have retired long ago but he discovered that he has not yet taken care of the needs of all the people. He is determined to continue going as long as possible. I admire the fact that in spite of his health situation these days, he nonetheless is determined to give all that he can. His love for God's people is limitless and so he goes about doing all that he can for as long as he can.

Dr. Graham is really a lesson for us all: none of us should give up. We should keep trying to serve because there is no greater joy than being a loving servant like Jesus our Savior is. Billy Graham came into the world and into the church when he was needed the most and now we will be needing more Billy Grahams in the years to come. I pray the Lord to reward him in time in this world and in eternity in the world to come.

Reverend Billy Graham, well done, good and faithful servant of Almighty God!

Patrick F. Flores was ordained as a Catholic priest in 1956. He has served as bishop of both San Antonio and El Paso, and is the current archbishop of San Antonio. He is a recipient of the Hispanic Heritage Award for leadership in the Hispanic community. Reverend Flores is a former chairman of the Church in Latin America Committee of the National Conference of Catholic Bishops.

Gerald R. Ford

On August 9, 1974, I assumed the world's most demanding office amidst the most dismal of circumstances. All too aware that I had not been elected to the presidency by the people's ballots, I asked my countrymen to confirm me in that position with their prayers. Among those who responded most generously was Billy Graham. I had known Billy throughout my congressional career. In fact, one of his earliest crusades took place in my hometown of Grand Rapids, Michigan. Over the years we had prayed together several times. I had benefited from his wise counsel.

Billy is a man whose love of country is second only to his love of God; for him, preaching and patriotism are indivisible. At the same time, he has never allowed national borders to stand as natural barriers. In this, as in so much else, he has been ahead of the politicians. To be perfectly honest, I initially entertained doubts when Billy ventured behind the Iron Curtain to preach the gospel in Soviet satellites whose record on human rights, including freedom of religion, was appalling. In the end, however, he proved himself to be a prophet with honor. Indeed, when the Berlin Wall finally came crashing down, I attributed

Billy Graham and President Gerald Ford
(photo courtesy of Gerald R. Ford Library)

no small part of the credit to Billy for planting seeds of faith in long-neglected soil. It was perhaps the greatest revival of his extraordinary career.

Of course, it's not only presidents who need to be prayed for, but ex-presidents as well. Twenty-five years after my East Room inaugural, I went back to Grand Rapids in August 1999, for a commemoration of the event. Honored as I was by such a tribute, I wanted the evening to be about much more than my years in the White House. To organizers, I expressed the hope that they would emphasize qualities of national character—including, of course, our faith in God and his providential care—that enabled us to surmount the Watergate crisis.

Billy Graham's presence in Grand Rapids that night transformed a historical anniversary into a joyous spiritual event. For him, the trip represented a very personal sacrifice. Truth be told, Billy's health was not what it had been. Only later did I learn that his beloved Ruth was in the hospital, undergoing tests and facing the prospect of surgery. How like Billy, I thought—one of the most selfless men I have ever known. Of course, Ruth has been a vital part of his life's work. Together they have brought the Good News to millions around the world.

The evening of August 19, 1999, was no exception. As a magnificent gospel choir from a local African-American church performed, we were caught up in the rousing music. This did not conceal the painful reality that it was difficult for Billy to be on his feet for more than a few minutes. When he approached the podium, however, the years seemed to fall away. A vigorous, spiritually robust man delivered a message of inspiration, without a written note, without a moment's pause or hesitation. It was pure Billy Graham, speaking from a heart inflamed with the love of Christ.

That's how I will always remember Billy: rising to the occasion, raising our own sights in the process, convinced of God's love and utterly convincing in explaining His purpose in our lives. America has been blessed in so many ways. Among our greatest blessings is this modern-day apostle who has never stopped reassuring us that we are all God's children. Bless you, Billy—for all you've done, for all you've been, and for all you are. America is in your debt.

I can think of no individual in the twentieth century (and now in the start of the twenty-first) who has so positively influenced as many lives as Reverend Billy Graham. His goal of helping others find and enjoy a personal relationship with Christ has led him around the world for more than half a century. His invitation to receive Christ has been extended to and received by individuals in every walk of life. I am grateful to Dr. Graham for the generous personal counsel he gave me during my presidency and in the years since.

Gerald R. Ford was elected to the U.S. House of Representatives in 1948 and reelected each term through 1972, serving twenty-five years in Congress. He became vice president in 1973 and served as the thirty-eighth president of the United States, from 1974 to 1977.

Robert A. Funk

Billy Graham brought me to Christ. It's simple to say. But that small sentence does not begin to convey what that has meant to my life. I had many good influences in my life and opportunities that came my way. But it was through my faith that I had the strength to take advantage of those opportunities.

I wonder how differently my life might have turned out had it not been for a revival in a Seattle stadium in September 1951. I was an eleven-year-old farm boy from the tiny town of Duvall, Washington, population two thousand. Church was a big part of my life and I looked forward to going to church with my mother and father. It was a time for socializing and spending time in Sunday school. I'd been going to church since I was ten days old. Mother tucked me in a shoebox that first Sunday under the back pew.

In September 1951, we heard Billy Graham was coming to do an outdoor revival in Seattle. This was only his third revival. He would be in Seattle for two whole weeks. Our pastor was participating in organizing the revival and he urged the whole congregation to attend. In those days, not everyone had cars in a town that size, and Seattle was almost an hour's drive—quite a distance for some. So the pastor rented buses to take the congregation to and from the revival each night. I went with my mother and sister every night.

It was a memorable experience for a young boy with knowledge of only a rural world. The stadium seemed gigantic to me. It had a seating capacity of eight thousand. Each day I watched people pour out of the stands by the hundreds to commit their lives to Jesus Christ. Billy Graham had a simple message. His style was new and different. He was not a fire-and-brimstone preacher threatening his parishioners with going to hell. He was sincere and direct and simply invited us to come down if we felt the Holy Spirit beckoning us.

Every night I listened to him. Every night, coming home on the bus, I would think the random thoughts that little boys have: "What if this?" "How come that?" One evening I thought to myself, "What if this bus crashed on the way home? Would I go to heaven?" I realized that even as a young boy, I was not prepared to meet my Maker. So that evening I decided to take the step of faith to be what Christ wanted me to be. When I went forward it was like my whole being was floating on air. I had been cleansed and given an opportunity to start fresh and clean with my relationship with Christ and my fellow man. In theological terms, it is called salvation and a quickened conscience.

It was an experience I will never forget. George Beverly Shea was the featured singer. He sang the powerful hymn that his rendition made one of the world's most popular: "How Great Thou Art." I went down with others and looked at Billy Graham up close and thought, "Wow, I am a Christian."

I have followed Billy Graham for fifty years. He remains one of my mentors, even though I have never spoken with him personally. Another hymn led by Cliff Barrows on that September day helped me to understand that Christ accepted me "Just as I Am." Through that experience my life has been forever changed and hopefully has influenced many others to change their lives.

Robert A. Funk founded Express Personnel Services in 1983. As the current chairman and CEO of Express Services, Inc., the parent company, he has helped Express Personnel Services spread into forty-six states and six countries. Mr. Funk is a member of the Board of Trustees for the International Franchise Association Educational Foundation.

Doris Greig

Many years ago I went to Mound, Minnesota, to teach home economics. I felt lonely but never thought of going to a church to get acquainted. I began to feel an emptiness and wondered if there was more to life. I didn't know any Christians and I had never been invited to a church. My family did not attend a church.

It was at this time that I met Bill Greig and started to date him. He was a good man and I liked being with him. However, when I was invited to have dinner at his parents' home I thought they had a very strange custom. After we ate, they would open up the Bible and read from it and discuss the passage. I had never read a Bible; I had only dusted the one Mom kept in our living room!

Bill's folks lived next door to the Keswick Conference Grounds. I had no idea what that was all about, but when they asked me if I would hostess in the dining hall, as Billy Graham was coming for a conference and they would be serving meals, I agreed because I wanted to get to know this Bill Greig better. I liked him and knew that he was a good man.

These meetings were for a Youth for Christ conference.

(After these meetings Billy Graham began to have large crusades.) They pitched a huge tent and had a week of meetings. Many people came, and Tim LaHaye helped park cars while I shooed people out of the dining hall so that they would get to the meeting on time.

The first night I went and heard the first gospel message that Billy Graham preached, I knew immediately what was missing from my life. I needed Jesus Christ to forgive my sins and to be my Lord and Savior. Now remember that I had not been in a church, and when Billy Graham invited people to come forward to receive Christ, I just couldn't move. I prayed the prayer as he led the people down in front. I remember that he said that if you had not come down in front to receive Christ, you could go home and kneel by your bed and invite Him into your life as your Lord and Savior. And that is exactly what I did that night when I returned to my little attic room where I was staying.

Life took in a new joy from that day forward. I always knew that there was something missing from my life, and now I knew who it was. I just thank the Lord that Bill Greig and his family invited me to their table and then to Billy Graham's meetings. I married Bill Greig about a year later and have had a wonderful life with four wonderful children that God entrusted to us. I have also been privileged to write the Joy of Living Bible Studies that are interdenominational studies used all over the U.S.

Doris Greig is the founder of Joy of Living, an organization that seeks to instruct individuals in the study of the Bible. She has written several of the Joy of Living courses and edited courses written by others. She is a member of the Joy of Living board of directors. Mrs. Greig is the author of We Didn't Know They Were Angels.

It was while I was a student at Wheaton College in Illinois that I heard that a young man named Billy Graham was to be speaking at Soldiers' Field in Chicago. I eagerly joined a group of fellow students who went to that huge stadium and sat mesmerized as Graham spoke.

Shortly after my husband, Jim Elliot, was killed by a tribe of jungle Indians in Ecuador I was visiting my parents in New Jersey. Billy called, inviting me to bring my two-year-old daughter, Valerie, to visit him and his wife in Montreat, North Carolina. That was an unforgettable experience to be a guest in their lovely mountaintop home.

Twice I was a speaker at the Intervarsity convention at the University of Illinois. Billy was the main speaker, and he asked me to have breakfast with him and others in order that he might question me regarding the roles of women—an issue very much in the forefront in those days of women's lib.

Perhaps the most delightful encounter I had with Billy and Ruth was an invitation from Johnny Cash to join them at his beautiful home in Jamaica. I'll never forget how heads spinned on the beach as bathers recognized those two well-known men strolling along the sand, deep in conversation.

Ruth Graham, Carole Carlson, Lars Gren, and Elisabeth Elliot Gren
(photo by Maury Scobee, courtesy of Elisabeth Elliot Gren)

I have been invited to the Grahams' home more times than I can count, and always greatly blessed. Thanks be to God for their steadfast following of the Lord Jesus.

Elisabeth Elliot Gren was born to missionary parents in Brussels, Belgium. She married missionary Jim Elliot in 1953. In 1956 Jim was killed by the Amazon's Auca Indians, to whom he and others were witnessing. Since then she has been writing and speaking around the world. Mrs. Gren has written several books including Shadow of the Almighty.

$\mathbf{M}$y wife, Mitzy, and I were invited to participate in one of the Billy Graham Crusades by giving a testimony of how God was operating in our young marriage and family. So with children Lonnie and Teresa in tow we headed excitedly for the crusade.

Since my mother-in-law was an admirer of Dr. Graham's ministry, we figured it would be meaningful to her if she could possibly meet with thousands of others who had the same dream. Circumstances fortunately allowed this to happen during the crusade. It was a thrill for all of us. From that moment, Dr. Graham and other members of the team would always ask about the family and inquire about Mitzy's mother, Mrs. Sloan, whenever we met.

Since that event, I've had the pleasure of singing in several of the crusades. I've always counted it a great honor to be on the same platform with Dr. Graham, Cliff Barrows, and George Beverly Shea.

The effectiveness of Dr. Graham's preaching and personal accountability over the years is well known. What do I say when someone asks me, "What is Billy Graham really like?" I simply tell them what I know from personal experience: he is a man who has no idea who he is or what an impact he has had on millions of lives around the world. But people like me, my family, and my mother-in-law surely do!

Larnelle Harris has brought home five Grammys, ten GMA Dove Awards, and more than a dozen number one records during his career as a modern gospel singer.

Morris Hatalsky

I first met Dr. Billy Graham at the Professional Golfers Association-sponsored tour event, the June 1977 Kemper Open, being played in Charlotte, North Carolina, Billy's birth city. My fellow golfer, Don Pooley, had invited me to attend a tour Bible study for about thirty golfers and family members at which Billy was speaking.

Even though Billy was famous and revered by millions, I was reluctant to attend. However, after more consideration and to appease my friend Don, I decided to go.

Little did I know that I would meet someone who would introduce me to Jesus Christ, who would literally transform my life. That evening, Billy's Bible message opened my eyes to God's truth of salvation—the gift of God's Son Jesus who died on a cross for my sins. He explained how Jesus bridged the gap between a holy God and sinful men just for me.

It was Billy Graham whom God used to deliver the incredible, penetrating message of love, grace, and judgment that overwhelmed me. To think that God loved me so much was beyond comprehension.

After Billy gave the invitation, I accepted God's gift of love and grace prayerfully and completely through Christ. I immediately went to Billy to thank him for his wonderful message of hope. He was so thoughtful and humble; I felt like I was talking to Jesus Himself!

I thank God for giving us this country preacher from North Carolina to speak to someone like me.

God bless you, Billy, for all eternity!

Morris Hatalsky has received much acclaim during his years on the PGA Tour. He has claimed victories at the Hall of Fame Classic (1981), the Greater Milwaukee Open (1983), the Kemper Open (1988), and the Bank of Boston Classic (1990). Mr. Hatalsky is cofounder of Trillium LLC and Trillium Links, a private country club course in North Carolina.

Mark O. Hatfield

Billy Graham has been a great blessing to me as well as to millions of other people over the life of his extraordinary ministry. I was too young to remember Billy Sunday, so I had no way to make comparisons to the one that came to be known as a world-famous evangelist.

My own background was that of being reared in a church where Sunday school and attendance to church activities were a way of life. But also, as a consequence, it became more of a cultural experience than a spiritual commitment. After serving in World War II, I came back to pick up my education and to pursue a political career. As a result, the early publicity relating to Billy Graham had not crossed my path. It was obvious that there was a tide of popularity surrounding this young man, and again, my activities of pursuing my career did not raise it high on my screen.

In 1957 I was in New York City at the same time that Graham was having his crusade in Madison Square Garden, and I decided to attend the final session in Times Square. Along with thousands of other people, I crowded into Times Square and he himself spoke from a center from which streets leading into the Square constituted this huge crowd. A public address system was provided for all of the side streets as well as the main street involved. I have to say I was greatly impressed to hear the man speak and preach the gospel, taking his text from the theater marquees to give it immediacy. One theater marquee portrayed the movie *Love from a Stranger,* and he took the word *love* and identified it from the biblical perspective—as God is love and his love was expressed in the sending of his son Jesus Christ. He related the true meaning of love, identifying it in a very dramatic way as something that was a gift and had to be received to be effective or meaningful.

I just by chance happened to run into another person of his crusade staff, and they invited me to meet him in person at a hotel where he was staying. I did, and again in retrospect it was not a matter of chance—I think it was preordained. Out of that first meeting and such, we became very good friends. I've supported his ministry from time to time, both financially and in prayer support.

There was a very interesting incident that occurred in my relationship and friendship with Billy Graham when Nixon was president. I was invited to speak at the National Prayer Breakfast at the time when the emotions and the feelings about the Viet Nam War were running very high, and I had the minority position of being a nonsupporter. In my remarks at the breakfast, in which Billy was a participant and sitting at the dais with President Nixon and others, I spoke on the subject of our priorities of life and referred to the war as "our national sin," because of my strong opposition to it. This was picked up by the media and a rather long article was written in the *New York Times*—and my remark was interpreted as a slap on the face of the president of the United States. Billy called me the next day and suggested that I ought to clarify that to depersonalize the statement as an effort not to embarrass the president, and so forth.

Billy and I remained very dear friends over the years, and we talked from time to time on political issues, particularly on the nuclear issue. I was so happy that Billy was very, very concerned about the nuclear arms race, and as you may remember, he eventually came to speak out in opposition to it.

Our other times together, where he was at our home for dinner and other occasions, were always very focused on the spiritual bond that brought us together and the spiritual ministry of his life. Naturally we talked political matters, but that was personal conversation that I have never quoted nor talked about in public. We had a confidential relationship on political matters, and in fact on all matters.

Billy Graham, to me, represented a resurgence after World War II of spiritual interest, spiritual concerns. He tapped in on that, representing it with consistency, quality, and integrity. And I think that he escaped all of the unfortunate negatives that often hit ministers or evangelists in high-profile positions because he was very astute at maintaining that integrity, both in the handling of financial matters, as well as his personal life. It makes me very proud to not only know him as a friend, but to appreciate the fact that he did have a tremendous impact on many people who would not otherwise have become active spiritually or have made their lives more spiritually meaningful were it not for him and his ministry. Many ministers came out of that experience of conversion in his crusades, and so it's a pleasure to say to you, "God bless Billy Graham," and I pray to God that he continues to have a very effective ministry.

Mark O. Hatfield has had a diverse career covering politics, the military, and education. A World War II veteran, he served as a professor of political science and dean of students at Willamette University before running for congressman in 1951. After serving as governor of Oregon, Mr. Hatfield served as senator from 1967 to 1997.

Dr. Jack Hayford

Recently, a curious personal encounter reminded me about what a remarkable gift the ministry of Billy Graham has been to the church around the world. This beloved and faithful evangelist has been both an anchor of reliability and a model of trustworthiness for over a half century of widespread ministry.

Why is Billy held in such consistently high esteem by virtually everyone in both the church and the secular community?

In light of the phenomenal trust and respect given Dr. Graham by the general public, I thought it worth closer examination. How did this leader establish patterns of conduct and ministry, both public and private, that have produced a track record of fidelity in every arena of life and service?

A rather unfruitful crusade in Modesto, California, in November 1948 turned out to be the catalyst that prompted the Graham team to set specific policies to help guard the ministry's integrity. The absence of community response to the crusade caused the team to seek God for reasons why.

The result of their open-hearted self-examination brought six major areas of concern into focus: money, sexual morality, sensationalism, hyperemotionalism, digressions into temporary

Billy Graham and Dr. and Mrs. Jack Hayford
(photo by T. Thorne Photography, courtesy of Dr. Jack Hayford)

emphases or issues, and insensitivity toward the entire body of Christ—particularly to its local pastors and churches.

Without taking time to sermonize or theorize on any of these points, let me simply amplify each by noting what is seen in Graham's ministry.

1. *Money.* Since the Billy Graham Evangelistic Association was formed in 1950, Billy has never accepted a love offering or an honorarium for work in his crusades. He would later accept

pay for his newspaper column and royalties from some of his books, but his salary for his evangelistic ministry was set.

He began with a salary of fifteen thousand dollars per year, a wage comparable to prominent urban pastors in this country. That same standard has continued to guide any upward adjustment.

2. *Sexual morality.* Candidly acknowledging their vulnerabilities to their own humanness and to the possibility of false appearances of wrongdoing, Billy and the team set strict, basic rules to protect themselves: (1) Keep in close proximity to one another on the road—recognizing the mutual strength of both partnership and accountability; and (2) never, for any reason, be alone with a woman, however pure the intent (as in counseling) or innocent the setting (as a ride to an auditorium or airport).

Together, the team would regularly pray: "Lord, guard us; keep us true and help us be sensitive in this area—even to keep from the appearance of evil."

3. *Sensationalism.* Any study of the preaching, writing, and evangelistic style of Billy Graham reveals a remarkable absence of the superficial, of hype, or of pandering to the crowd or playing to the grandstands. Even in the early years, when his own youthfulness and his beginnings as a youth evangelist showed up in a more dramatic delivery, his communication consistently avoided exaggeration or slick remarks. There's never been anything cutesy or clever about his style. There are no grandiose claims or stunts employed to attract attention.

4. *Hyperemotionalism*. It is interesting to observe Billy Graham's balance in this respect. As both an evangelical and a Pentecostal, I have been encouraged by his steadfast maintenance of a middle road between the extremes of intellectualized sophistry and emotionalistic folderol. He is not afraid to confront people with the eternal issues of heaven's promise and hell's judgment, yet I've never heard him become either syrupy on the one hand or mean on the other. The plaintive strains of "Just As I Am" are a hallmark of his altar calls, but this unabashed use of so heart-touching an approach is employed without apology.

His recognition that the Holy Spirit does move upon human emotions is balanced by his commitment to let *Him* draw people to Christ. Graham merely bows in prayer while seekers come forward—moved by God, without a manipulative appeal.

5. *Avoiding digressions*. Billy Graham has written on prophecy, yet he has never been caught in the trap of sign-seeking, date-setting, or charting the future and putting it up for sale. He has been at the center of our nation's moral and civic consciousness, having counseled presidents and called the country to obey God's laws. Yet he's never been snagged by a single political party and hasn't allowed himself to digress into any special focus on one political, moral, or doctrinal issue.

"The Bible says . . ." has been his badge of authority and the bedrock of his ministry. There is not a sector of the church that hasn't been touched by his breadth of ministry. He hasn't allowed himself to be crowded into narrow corners of emphasis that would preclude him from being a blessing to all.

6. *Commitment to the whole church.* Billy Graham set a style that rescued the possibility of gaining some semblance of unity in the America church. He insisted that all churches and church leaders would be welcome—indeed solicited and encouraged— to be involved in his crusades. From Congregationalists to Methodists, from Presbyterians to Conservative Baptists, and from Adventists to Catholics—all were received as partners for the sake of evangelism.

This largesse toward the whole body of Christ is also seen in Graham's commitment to the local church and in his love for pastors and church leaders. Cliff Barrows sums up his partner's attitude toward local church leaders: "He genuinely loves them and has sought to learn all he can from them instead of criticizing their ministry. He tries to be sympathetic with the problems they face."

I was in my early teen years when Billy Graham's name became nationally renowned. I've met him, conversed with him in the circle of small groups of pastors, and have been privileged to be invited to minister in the schools of evangelism he sponsors.

Although I've never been a close friend or confidant I, like a multitude of other pastors and church leaders, have been profoundly influenced by his model of manliness, morality, and clarity in message.

Psalm 37:37 says: "Mark the blameless man, and observe the upright; for the future of that man is peace."

Being instructed by that exhortation from God's Word, it's helpful to have so ready a point of reference for follow-through.

Thank you, Lord, for a man named Billy.

Dr. Jack Hayford is perhaps best known as founding pastor of The Church on the Way in Van Nuys, California. Additionally he founded The Kings College and Seminary, the Jack W. Hayford School of Pastoral Nurture, and Living Way Ministry, whose teaching cassettes are distributed worldwide. Dr. Hayford is the author of more than three dozen books including How to Live Through a Bad Day.

Jesse Helms

I t was the early 1950s that Billy Graham's divine purpose in this world suddenly became clear to me. I do not claim that it was a revelation accompanied by bugles and drums; I had of course heard of Billy Graham off and on but I cannot claim a previous awareness that this man was destined for an incredible impact on mankind.

I believe it was on a Sunday in 1952. I had taken a job as administrative assistant in Washington to a fine U.S. senator, Willis Smith. I had accepted the job reluctantly; my wife, Dot, and I had been blessed with two little daughters and I disliked the idea of leaving them in Raleigh while I was 260 miles away trying to serve a senator. The best I could do was commute to and from Washington every other weekend. I had a room with two wonderful elderly ladies in their apartment on 14th Street.

My Sundays in Washington were routine: church and sometimes Sunday school in the morning, a quick lunch, then to the Capitol, where I always had plenty of paperwork catching-up to do.

One Sunday morning I noted a small item in *The Washington Star* that evangelist Billy Graham would conduct a crusade that afternoon on the steps of the U.S. Capitol.

Billy Graham and Senator Jesse Helms
(photo courtesy of Senator Jesse Helms)

I confess apprehension that only a relative few might show up. So instead of going to my desk in the Capitol, I went to the Capitol grounds fearing, as I say, that only a handful might be on hand.

Well, as I approached, I heard—before I saw—the three acres of people who had gathered to worship with Billy

Graham. I recall thanking the Lord that so many had come for what proved to be a powerful sermon by Dr. Billy Graham.

The next day, Senator Smith hosted a luncheon in Dr. Billy Graham's honor to which several other senators and a couple of staff people had been invited.

It was then that the enormity of Billy Graham's service to our Lord became clear to me and it was then that my personal relationship with Billy and his remarkable wife, Ruth, began.

Since then, there have been countless instances when Dot and I have been blessed with their friendship and guidance. There have been so many telephone conversations, so many personal visits in our respective homes—plus the fact that our two daughters have been close friends with Ann Graham Lotz and her husband, Danny, and their children.

I shall not dwell on our personal blessings except to mention that the Lotz family and the Helms family were members of the same church in Raleigh where Annie began her first ministry. Suffice it to say that all of these relationships have been blessings to our family. There have been times when I hope we have been of some small assistance to the various Grahams.

I do know what all of them, starting with Billy and Ruth, have meant to Dot and me. Never a day passes that we don't thank the Lord for the blessing that Billy and Ruth Graham have been to us and to so many millions of others throughout the world. They are truly messengers for God.

Senator Jesse Helms served his first term in the Senate in 1973, representing North Carolina. He is chairman of the Committee on Foreign Relations; a member of the Committee on Agriculture, Nutrition, and Forestry; and a member of the Rules Committee. After a long and industrious career in Washington, Senator Helms has announced his decision to retire after his present term.

It was June 1972 and almost one hundred thousand young believers filled the Cotton Bowl in Dallas on a sweltering Friday night to hear Dr. Billy Graham close the massive evangelism training event Explo '72. One of the participants listened intently to every word the legendary evangelist spoke as he simply but powerfully explained the power of one person to change the world. Dr. Graham ended his message by having the stadium lights turned off and then lighting a single candle from the podium, from which a second candle was lighted. The two candles then became four and continued to multiply until almost one hundred thousand candles illuminated the stadium with such a glow that nearby residents called the Dallas Fire Department to report the Cotton Bowl was on fire.

And it was!

Sparks of that spiritual fire kindled something in the life of that young man from Hope, Arkansas. He was not yet seventeen years old and would soon start his senior year of high school. The week before Explo '72, that young man had been elected governor of Arkansas Boys State, a program to encourage young people in politics. Twenty-four years later, that same young man would be sworn in as the forty-fourth governor of Arkansas, and Billy Graham would still be influencing his life.

That young man was me.

I had heard Billy Graham's sermons on radio and television since I was a child. Even my father, who had only trusted Christ the summer before in 1971, would give ear to Dr. Graham's compelling messages during my childhood. As a teenager, I read books by Dr. Graham and used a devotional guide he had written for my daily quiet time. But hearing him in person was a privilege I thought I would never have.

God spoke to me in a powerful way that summer night in 1972. Though I had been a believer since age ten, Dr. Graham's message that night on the importance of being the "light of the world" would start a process of spiritual discovery for me that continues to this day.

Since the 1940s Billy Graham has been the "gold standard" of Christian evangelism. His ministry has been the model for all ministries. Few people in Christian history have had more critics and character assassins than Billy Graham. The attempts to discredit him have always fallen short.

Through the years, millions have started on the road to heaven because of Billy Graham. Only in heaven will we fully know the impact of his ministry. Behind the numbers are people who have a personal story of a life touched and turned toward Christ. For that sixteen-year-old high school kid from Arkansas, it made all the difference.

Mike Huckabee served as pastor and president of Cambridge Communications in Texarkana and as president of Arkansas Baptist State convention before assuming the governorship of Arkansas in 1996. He is currently chairman of the Southern Growth Policies Board and serves on the executive committee of the National Governors' Association. Mr. Huckabee has written three books including Character Is the Issue.

Dr. John A. Huffman

The year was 1946. The place was a resort on Boston's North Shore. The purpose was a gathering of all the founding leadership of the young organization named Youth for Christ. The host was my father, who in addition to pastoring a church in Cambridge and working on his doctorate at Harvard, was the New England director of Youth for Christ, leading the rally every Saturday night at the historic Part Street Congregational Church in Boston.

Attending that meeting was a young evangelist named Billy Graham, the vice president at large for that fledgling organization. And also present at the meeting was a six-year-old youngster who tagged along to the proceedings with his father and mother and kid sister. I was that six-year-old.

I'm not certain quite how it happened. But somehow that tall, lanky evangelist in his late twenties took a liking to me, tossed me around in the air, and took me for a walk along the sandy beach and a climb over some of the boulders on that ragged New England coast. I don't remember one word that was said. But I remember being drawn to this contagious person who from that moment on impacted my life in such positive ways.

My next contact with Billy Graham was a couple of years later when I watched as my father, Dr. Harold John Ockenga, and Billy Graham met in the living room of our summer home in Winona Lake, Indiana. Dr. Ockenga was inviting this still obscure Billy Graham to come and hold some evangelistic services in Boston at the earliest possible date. Graham accepted the invitation and continued westward to Los Angeles to that crusade in which he would gain such national prominence.

I can still remember my father's surprise when he and I were driving in the car one evening, listening to his favorite newscaster, Lowell Thomas. Thomas referred to a young evangelist holding meetings in Los Angeles to which thousands were thronging and many, including celebrities, were coming to faith in Jesus Christ. My father could not believe his ears when I said, "Dad, that's your friend Billy Graham." My dad, who had not been listening carefully, responded, "No, John, you don't understand. There's a boxer by the name of Billy Graham. No friend of mine would ever be important enough to by mentioned by Lowell Thomas on the news." It wasn't much later that Billy Graham arrived in Boston for those two mid-century crusades held in back-to-back years that outgrew Park Street Church, Mechanics Hall, and even the Boston Garden with that great Sunday afternoon rally in which fifty thousand people withstood the rain showers to hear the Gospel preached.

Our paths crossed again when I attended the final rally of the New York crusade in Yankee Stadium in the mid-fifties. He spoke at my graduation from Wheaton College in 1962 and came to Princeton Seminary and University, addressing both student bodies during my graduate days there in the early sixties. And I've been blessed by frequent visits with him when he's attended churches I've served. I've attended crusades and congresses on evangelism that he's led. We've played golf together. We've been mutually engaged in seminars and National Prayer Breakfasts and have served together on the boards of Gordon-Conwell Theological Seminary and Christianity Today, Inc.

I'm now in my early sixties, over a half century older than when I first met Dr. Graham. Although he was not the influence God used to lead me to Jesus Christ, he has been a steadying influence throughout my entire life, from that first meeting to the present. Throughout these years it has been his integrity that has meant the most to me. He's always endeavored to be faithful to God's Word, the Bible, and has endeavored to graciously witness to the person and work of Jesus Christ no matter how secular the environment in which he found himself. Frankly, I have made it a point to try to touch base with some aspect of Billy Graham's ministry on an annual basis as a means of reminding myself of the importance of evangelistic fervor, personal integrity, and a straightforward winsomeness in the presentation of the Gospel. Billy Graham has helped me maintain my priorities and a Christ-centered focus! Billy Graham has meant so much to me as a personal friend and a spiritual model.

Dr. John A. Huffman Jr. has been the pastor of the 4,500-member St. Andrew's Presbyterian Church in California since 1978. He is currently chairman of the board of World Vision U.S. and serves on several other boards such as National Council of the Churches of Christ in the U.S.A., Gordon-Conwell Theological Seminary, and Christianity Today, Inc.

Jerry B. Jenkins

Being asked to assist Billy Graham with his memoirs, *Just As I Am,* resulted in the privilege of a lifetime.

As anyone who has spent significant blocks of time with Mr. Graham would attest, I found him the same behind closed doors as in public. What some might call his star quality—that aspect that seems to light a room and attract people (and the spotlight) to him, is ironically born of humility.

Assuming the typical reader would want to know what makes Mr. Graham the Christian he is, one day in his office in Montreat, North Carolina, I tried to get him to talk about it. My first several attempts failed. I said, "Most evangelicals see you as the epitome of . . ."

He frowned and held up a hand. "They shouldn't see me as the epitome of anything."

"But they do," I said. "Some would consider you the Protestant Pope, and—"

"You know," Mr. Graham said, "sometimes I feel this low"—and here he leaned from his chair and put his palm flat on the floor— "when I think of the number of times I've failed the Lord."

Billy Graham and Jerry B. Jenkins
(photo courtesy of Jerry B. Jenkins)

Here was the man many of us have put on a pedestal, held up as an example of the believer in word and deed, regretting his inconsistencies. How was I going to find some takeaway value for the common Christian from the life of this leader if he insisted on emphasizing his weaknesses rather than his strengths?

I circled the issue a few more times, clearly troubling him

more each time: "People really should not look to me as an example."

Finally I stumbled onto a question he would answer. "How do you maintain your own spiritual disciplines?"

"There's no secret to that," Mr. Graham said. "God makes it plain and simple in the Bible. We are to pray without ceasing and search the Scriptures."

"You pray without ceasing?" I said, having always hoped the Apostle Paul's admonition was less literal than it seemed.

"I do," Mr. Graham said. "And I have nearly every waking moment since I received the Lord as a teenager. I'm praying right now that our conversation will bring glory to God and that this book project will be worthy of our efforts."

I was stunned. "And what form does your searching the Scriptures take?"

"Wherever I am in the world," he said, "whether it be here or at home or in a hotel or at someone's house, I place my open Bible where I will see it frequently. Whenever I notice it I stop and read a verse or two or a chapter or two or even for an hour or two. This is not for sermon preparation or study. This is just for my spiritual nourishment—my food."

I sat back and was moved to notice just over his shoulder his open Bible on the corner of his desk. Still, I worried I was not gleaning anything transferable to everyday believers who long to be consistent in their daily walks. "What do you do when you miss a day or two?" I tried.

Mr. Graham cocked his head and pressed his lips together. "Oh, I don't think I've ever done that," he said. "I told you, it's my spiritual food. I don't miss meals."

As I drove back to my hotel that day, I worried that I had not dug up anything that made Mr. Graham and his victorious faith any more accessible to the average Christian. But then it hit me, what it was that set him apart. As he said, it was no secret. God does not hide it from us. He tells us to pray without ceasing and to search the Scriptures.

What sets Mr. Graham apart as a man of God is not some super power within himself, some character trait that elevates him. What makes him who he is and results in his ministry being blessed seemingly above so many others' similar work is that Mr. Graham does it. He prays without ceasing and searches the Scripture—something we can all do, if we simply would.

Jerry B. Jenkins, former vice president for publishing and currently writer-at-large for the Moody Bible Institute of Chicago, is the author of more than one hundred books and he co-authored with Dr. Tim LaHaye the bestselling Left Behind series. He is also the former editor of Moody Magazine. Mr. Jenkins assisted Dr. Graham with his bestselling memoirs, Just As I Am.

Dr. D. James Kennedy

One of my most memorable experiences with Billy Graham dates back to February 3, 1974, when he came to Fort Lauderdale to dedicate the brand new Coral Ridge Presbyterian church building, "What a gorgeous and glorious church you are going to have—physically and spiritually," he said to me personally at that time. Then, during his address to the congregation, he shared his sparkling humor with a gentle warning against getting too proud of the new facilities, quoting an anonymous clergyman who was supposed to have said, "If I ever see a humble Presbyterian, I'll be like Moses—I will turn aside to see this great sight."

"I hope that this congregation will not forget," he continued in a serious vein, "that it was born just a few years ago, forty-five or fifty people—people who loved the Lord, who believed in prayer and believed in evangelism. And you went out, and you have done something that has become a twentieth-century phenomenon in the kingdom of God. The example of this church is being followed by churches all over the world, and your responsibility is so much greater than the average congregation."

It is that kind of perceptive and good-natured intimacy that make people from all levels of society around the globe feel so close to this great man who expresses himself in simple and sincere terms to which they can immediately relate.

What can be said of such a universally loved and respected man of God that has not already been articulated by some of the most eloquent spokespersons, not only in Christendom, but in religions outside of the household of faith? People are generally inclined to liken Billy Graham to the Christ he so passionately preaches—and to whose image he has been conformed.

Perhaps the apostle John said it for us best: "We love him because he first loved us."

Dr. D. James Kennedy is senior minister of the nearly ten-thousand-member Coral Ridge Presbyterian Church in Fort Lauderdale. He is founder and president of Evangelism Explosion International, the first ministry to be established in every nation on the earth, as well as founder of the Center for Christian Statesmanship and the Center for Reclaiming America. Dr. Kennedy has authored more than forty-five books.

Dr. Billy (Jang Hwan) Kim

Billy Graham is a friend who has portrayed a godly example with his heart for evangelism, his love for the Word of God, his lifestyle of integrity, and his humility. He is a choice servant of God.

Dr. Billy Kim and Billy Graham
(photo courtesy of Dr. Billy Kim)

He is not only concerned about the public propagation of the gospel, but also interested in the individual person. Ruth's work on behalf of the welfare and well being of the family has certainly been a significant complement to Dr. Graham's ministry.

One of the most memorable events of my life and ministry was the opportunity to interpret for Dr. Billy Graham at the 1973 Korean Crusade where more than one million people attended a single service.

Dr. Billy Kim is a pastor, evangelist, and broadcaster. He currently serves as senior pastor of the fifteen-thousand-member Suwon Central Baptist Church in Suwon, Korea, as well as the president of the Far East Broadcasting Company in Korea. Dr. Kim is currently serving a five-year term as president of the Baptist World Alliance.

The author of Hebrews commands us to, "Remember your leaders, who spoke the word of God to you. Consider the outcome of their way of life and imitate their faith" (Heb. 13:7). For over sixty years, Reverend Graham has been speaking the Word of God to all of us, calling nonbelievers to repentance and believers to endurance.

Consider the outcome: long before I met Billy, when I shared at a crusade in Tacoma, Washington, I admired his leadership and integrity. His life and ministry are incomparable; perhaps no man has been used by God to draw more people to himself.

The apostle Paul says that God uses simple "jars of clay" to deliver His priceless message (2 Cor. 4). Dr. Graham is one such vessel, holding out the message of Jesus in plainspoken ways and waiting for the Holy Spirit to move in people's hearts. As a public figure, he has been the Christian community's standard-bearer for years. When met with worldly acclaim and popularity, Dr. Graham's response to God's blessing has been prayerful humility and faithful perseverance. Even in the era of profiteering preachers, Dr. Graham's commitment to personal integrity makes him beyond reproach.

"Imitate their faith." Greater than the challenge Dr. Graham makes from the pulpit, is the challenge he makes with his life. If one wonders what it looks like to follow the call of Christ, he doesn't need to look farther than Billy Graham. His is a faith worth imitating.

Steve Largent is currently serving his third term representing Oklahoma in Congress. In his fourteen years with the Seattle Seahawks, he set six different career records and participated in seven Pro Bowls. In 1995 Mr. Largent was inducted into the Pro Football Hall of Fame.

Dr. Roy B. McKeown

What has Billy Graham meant to me? My answer to this question is many-faceted, simply because this remarkable man has been a very vital part of my life and ministry for many years. Let me explain.

Billy Graham has been a showcase for Jesus Christ, not only for me and many other young preachers like myself, but for my wife of fifty-six years, our children, and our exciting grandchildren as well. He has been a faithful friend and mentor and has served as the example of a dedicated Christian life.

Billy has constantly provided leadership for me to follow. He is always the inspiration for my own messages, with his consistent, "The Bible says . . ." The simplicity of his preaching has been my guide, as over and over I've heard him say, "The only way to go to heaven is through Jesus Christ."

To digress. . . I first met Billy Graham—this tall, lanky, handsome young man—at a Youth for Christ conference in Winona Lake, Indiana. I was young, extremely enthusiastic, and very much in love with Jesus Christ. You could even say that I was "on fire for the Lord" as I served as director of the Los Angeles Youth for Christ, and I loved serving as a delegate to the conference.

Billy Graham and Dr. Roy B. McKeown
(photo courtesy of Dr. Roy B. McKeown)

Now the year was August 1948 and the place was Beaten-
berg, Switzerland. This was the first Youth for Christ International Worldwide Congress. Again, I was a thrilled delegate,
and Billy was the keynote speaker. I didn't know Billy well at
that time, but when he began to speak, I was captivated and
overwhelmed. My dad, a pastor, accompanied me to this event,
and as Billy delivered the keynote address, Dad whispered to

me: "Roy, as sure as I live, God is going to use that young man!"

Now the year was 1949, and I was honored to serve on the committee for the Greater Los Angeles Billy Graham Crusade. The publisher of the *Los Angeles Examiner,* impressed by this young evangelist, sent out the order in newspaper jargon: "Puff Graham!" And as the word went out to the many Hearst papers, more and more people began pouring into that great big tent to hear this fiery, dynamic preacher. Yes, the Billy Graham crusades were born!

Night after night, those of us on the executive committee would meet with Billy and pray under that canvas ceiling for God's anointing on the evening's sermon. The dates of the crusade were extended . . . it went on for weeks. And I have never been the same since. He gave me a burning desire to reach a world for Christ.

In 1960 I was invited to head up the Capital Teen Convention in Washington, D.C., which was attended by some ten thousand teenagers from all over the world. Once again, Billy was the keynote speaker and as we worked together on this exciting event, I was again impressed by the humility of this man who was, by now, world-famous . . . yet he cared only to be known as God's servant.

As no other man in history has done, Billy Graham opened the door for evangelical ministry to a world that didn't have the slightest idea what being "born again" meant. And over the years, this basic, fundamental message has remained the same, spoken by a man of incredible humility. No wonder God has used him!

Just last Sunday I listened to Billy preach, and I felt my eyes fill with tears as he again proclaimed Jesus Christ his Lord and Savior. In his senior years, he is still as powerful as he was when I first heard him. Has he impacted my life? Yes, beyond anything or anyone else!

Dr. Roy B. McKeown began his career as director of Los Angeles Youth for Christ and was later appointed vice president of Youth for Christ International for the West Coast. He is founder and president of World Opportunities International, a Christian humanitarian organization with worldwide outreach. A recipient of numerous awards, Dr. McKeown is the author of Desperate Street.

Dr. Billy A. Melvin

My first contact with Billy Graham came in the mid-1950s when he came to Richmond, Virginia, for an evangelistic crusade. I was pastoring a church in the city and led my congregation in full support of the crusade.

Little did I realize at the time that in the providence of God I was to have a long and cordial association with Billy Graham. It began in the late 1960s and spanned three decades while I was serving as the executive director of the National Association of Evangelicals (NAE). Since the histories of the Billy Graham Evangelistic Association (BGEA) and NAE parallel one another, there were common concerns and aspirations that bound us together.

The special times for me were those occasions when Billy would come to address the annual NAE convention. Whatever the trends of the day, he would always have a timely word and remind us that faithfulness in proclaiming the gospel message was the order of the day.

During those visits, it was often my privilege to sit next to Billy during the banquet meal that preceded his message. Each time it seemed like we would pick up our conversation from the last time—two friends talking as if they had never parted!

Billy Melvin and Billy Graham
(photo courtesy of Billy Melvin)

I especially remember his visit to our convention in 1992 when we were celebrating the fiftieth anniversary of NAE. Both of us were in somewhat of a reflective mood as we realized that time was quickly passing and the energy of youth was fading. I don't remember his exact words—it has been a while—but I do remember the impression I carried away that night. It was this: whatever time God may give us, we must fulfill our calling and be faithful.

I am grateful for Billy's reminder that evening and the example of faithfulness he has been to the Christian community.

Billy A. Melvin served twenty-eight years as executive director of the National Association of Evangelicals. He is president and CEO of Church Consulting Services, Inc. Dr. Melvin is a cofounder of the Christian Association of PrimeTimers, a ministry to Christian seniors.

Dr. Stephen Olford

I have known Dr. Billy Graham for over fifty years. From our first meeting at Hildenborough Hall in southern England in October 1946 we were bonded in the Spirit. This was a conference center established by evangelist Tom Rees where hundreds of young people converged for holidaymaking and biblical teaching. I had spent the whole week sharing what I had learned from the Word of God concerning the work of the Holy Spirit in a believer's life—and there was revival! At the end of that week who should arrive from the United States but Torrey Johnson, Chuck Templeton, Billy Graham, Cliff Barrows, Stratton Shufelt, and one or two others. As was the custom, there was a testimony meeting on the last night. Then, to close the program, I preached on Ephesians 5:18. God came down in power. Tom Rees said, "All who want dealings with God, who have not already come into blessing, go into the chapel. We are going to give Stephen Olford twenty minutes to rest." I sat there with my head bowed.

Suddenly I sensed a presence before me. I looked up and I saw this handsome, tall young man, Billy Graham. I can visualize him now in his light suit, sporting an impossible tie! He said, "Why didn't you give an invitation?"

Dr. Stephen Olford, President Richard Nixon, and Billy Graham
(photo courtesy of Stephen Olford / Olford Ministries International)

I said, "An invitation has been given. In twenty minutes I'll be meeting with all those who really want to know how to be filled with the Spirit. Why did you ask?"

He said, "I would have been the first to come forward. I don't know anything about this in my life."

He was unable to stay. He was going . . . to Wales. We made a date to meet in the Welsh town of Pontypridd in Taff Vale, only eleven miles from my home, where Billy was having some meetings . . . I found that Billy was seeking for more of God with all his heart, and he felt that I could help him. For most of two days we were closeted at Pontypridd's hotel with our Bibles open, turning the pages as we studied passages and verses. The first day Billy learned more secrets of the "quiet time." The next I expounded the fullness of the Holy Spirit in the life of a believer who is willing to bow daily and hourly to the sovereignty of Christ and to the authority of the Word. This lesson was so new to me that it cascaded out, revealing bright glimpses of the inexhaustible power of the love of God.

Billy drank it in so avidly that I scarcely realized the heights and depths that his spiritual life had reached already. At the close of the second day we prayed, like Jacob of old laying hold of God, and crying, "Lord, I will not let Thee go except Thou bless me," until we came to a place of rest and rejoicing. And Billy Graham said, "This is a turning point in my life. This will revolutionize my ministry."

If I were to sum up the secret of his greatness, I would liken him to Joshua, after the death of Moses. Having responded in total surrender to the call of God to lead Israel into the Promised Land, "the Lord said to Joshua, 'This day I will begin to magnify you in the sight of all [people]'" (Joshua 3:7). This is what has happened to my dear colleague Billy Graham. Most of the world has been impacted in one way or another by his preaching, testimony, and influence.

Three outstanding features have characterized his life and ministry:

1. *His Christlike Humility.* Rarely have I met a man so eulogized and publicized who, at the same time, was so humble. I have prayed with him alone on numerous occasions and have been broken in spirit as I sensed his genuine humility. It is because of this discipline and disposition of meekness that God has exalted him in great power and fame.

2. *His Christlike Simplicity.* This is the hallmark of his preaching. Men and women, boys and girls, scholars and simple folk understand the gospel when he preaches. Like his Master before him it can be said, "The common people [literally "the huge crowd"] go on listening to him gladly."

3. *His Christlike Authority.* From the moment Billy Graham accepted by faith the Bible as the inerrant Word of God, he has had an anointed authority in his preaching. When he declares "The Bible says" people listen. His authority derives from his unflinching commitment to the trustworthiness of God's Word. So untold multitudes have turned to faith in Christ because "faith comes by hearing, and hearing by the word of God" (Rom. 10:17).

My life has been immeasurably enriched by this dear man of God.

Stephen Olford is founder of Olford Ministries International and senior lecturer at the Stephen Olford Center for Biblical Preaching. He has served as minister of both Duke Street Baptist Church in Richmond, Surrey, England, and the famed Calvary Baptist Church in New York City. Dr. Olford has authored numerous books.

Dr. Juan Carlos Ortiz

My first contact with Dr. Billy Graham was when I heard him on *The Hour of Decision* forty-three years ago by short-wave radio on HCJB aired from Quito, Ecuador, while planting a church in a distant place of the Córdoba Hills of Argentina. Later I saw him at a large crusade in Montevideo, Uruguay, and in Buenos Aires, Argentina. Then I was invited by his organization to be one of the speakers at the first Congress of Evangelization in Lausanne, Switzerland, in 1974.

One of the things that impressed me the most about this man of God is the loyalty and fidelity in his team. Since I met him, until today, he has been surrounded by the same people. Any person can be a friend for a time, but to achieve this kind of friendship, loyalty, fidelity, and unity in a team for so long speaks very highly of a leader. To be always faithful is a divine quality in a team, like the Holy Trinity.

Another important quality of his person and ministry is stability. Never an unpleasant surprise! His walk with God has always been stable, continued, and consequent. This spiritual growth is noticed in his publications and in all phases of his ministry.

People close to him describe him as very humble—how he will confess to God his sins in front of his team, in spite of being such a famous person, always depending on the merits of Christ and not on his own dignity or personality. This is a very strong lesson to me.

Another thing that has impressed me is his desire and effort to multiply his life forming other evangelists and motivating pastors with the evangelistic zeal. Certainly Billy Graham has been one of the most fruitful and influential ministers for the Kingdom of God.

While speaking at the Congress on Evangelization at Lausanne, Switzerland, Dr. Robert H. Schuller was present, heard me speak, and in 1990 invited me to be part of the Crystal Cathedral Ministries. Thanks to this connection, today there's a strong Hispanic ministry functioning at the Crystal Cathedral. I'm sure there must be many more of these connections throughout the world because of Billy Graham's ministry.

Dr. Juan Carlos Ortiz is founder and pastor of the Hispanic ministry at the Crystal Cathedral with Dr. Robert H. Schuller. Born in Buenos Aires, he has founded six churches, including the largest evangelical church in Buenos Aires from 1966 to 1978. For several years he produced the Latin American TV show La Hora de Poder *(The Hour of Power). Dr. Ortiz has written several books including* God Is Closer Than You Think.

Humility coupled with love has to be the top characteristic of a servant leader. No one has made that more real to me than Dr. Billy Graham.

Years ago, I was invited to speak at a youth congress in Essen, Germany. Billy Graham was there, too, and I happened to be visiting with Dr. Graham in his hotel room when a German evangelist came for an interview.

This German was a sharp evangelist with a growing team, but he had one problem: nobody invited him to have crusades. Mr. Graham gave him a few ideas, the German asked a few more questions, and we all got on our knees to pray.

Mr. Graham began pouring out his heart for this evangelist, asking God to bless him. When his voice became muffled, I thought, "What's he doing?" I opened my eyes to see Billy flat on his face in front of the German. Not on all fours, but straight-out flat, face down, on the floor!

After the man said good-bye, Mr. Graham said to me, "You know, Luis, the Bible says, 'Humble yourselves under the mighty hand of God' (1 Peter 5:6). I believe the best thing for an evangelist is to humble himself every day, even physically. I pray a lot flat on my face. In due time, He will raise us up!"

Luis Palau and Billy Graham
(photo courtesy of Luis Palau)

You want to know the secret of why God has used Billy Graham to preach the Gospel to more people in live audiences than anyone else in history? Because he humbles himself every day in obedience to Scripture. I will be indebted forever for his example.

In 1966 Luis Palau held his first evangelistic campaign in Bogotá, Columbia. A year later he was named Overseas Crusade's Latin

America Field Director and in 1978 he left to form the Luis Palau Evangelistic Association. Mr. Palau has written numerous books including The Only Hope for America.

Ruth Stafford Peale

I was the wife of a pastor serving a church on Fifth Avenue in New York City when, years ago, Billy Graham had a crusade in a large auditorium in our city. I attended many of those services and often sat with Ruth Graham, his wife. She was sometimes in a front row in this great auditorium. At other times she chose a seat in the huge balcony.

Ruth Graham was a spiritual partner as well as a wife. She was beautiful—always tastefully groomed, friendly and approachable. It was apparent that she had Billy in her prayers all through each service. Then she would volunteer to meet with many who came forward as Billy gave the invitation for any who would accept Christ to come forward. I am sure that Billy Graham felt the influence of his wonderful wife. They are a great team. And they both were a great inspiration to me.

Ruth Stafford Peale is founder and publisher of Guideposts, *which publishes five magazines that have a combined paid circulation of 4.5 million. She is the author of the book* Secrets of Staying in Love *and oversaw the publication of the notes and quotations of her late husband,* Norman Vincent Peale, *in the* Positive Thinking Bible.

Sir Cliff Richard

It's probably unfashionable these days to admit to having heroes but, quite unashamedly, I confess that Dr. Billy Graham is mine.

From the first time I heard him preach, way back in the mid-1960s, I admired his courage, his faith, and his style. As I got to know him over subsequent years, admiration developed into a huge respect as I recognized his dedication and unswerving integrity. It's been that integrity, of course, that has fazed and silenced would-be cynics and critics and has led to his unique standing in the Christian world.

One seemingly trivial incident spoke volumes to me about Billy's commitment. After one of his mission meetings in England, I was invited back to his hotel for a brief meeting. Billy was resting in his room, and I couldn't help noticing that, while we spoke, he was all the time gripping a length of rough wood. I probably didn't hide my curiosity too well, because after a while he explained that he carried the wood with him on his travels to exercise his hand and particularly his grip. He had some arthritis in his fingers and didn't want to end up having to offer a "wet fish" handshake, which he felt was disrespectful and gave a weak impression.

That lesson in personal discipline and attention to detail has remained with me ever since. For Billy Graham, Jesus is no limp-wristed sentimentalist, but instead strong, relevant, uncompromising, and attractive. And, if that's the Jesus we represent, that's the Jesus we must strive to be.

Sir Cliff Richard has had a record 117 hit singles during his career in pop music, a feat no other British band or soloist has come even close to matching. He was knighted by Queen Elizabeth II during the 1995 Birthday Honours for his charity work.

Bobby Richardson

One of Billy Graham's very first crusades was in my home-town in South Carolina. I didn't get to attend because I had a paper route and duties of delivering. Shortly after that my pastor led me to Christ. I signed out of high school with the New York Yankees and as a twenty-year-old was able to attend Billy Graham's long-running crusade at Madison Square Garden in New York with some of my Yankee teammates. Larry McPhail, former owner of the Dodgers and later the Yankees, attended and turned his life over to Christ.

And then I was humbled and honored to be asked to share my testimony in crusades in Houston at the Astrodome with President Johnson in attendance and later in Honolulu, Hawaii, and Japan with national coverage. In fact, Cliff Barrows held up a copy of my autobiography on national television and said, "You should get a copy," and it sold over one hundred thousand copies and was used to influence many to Christ.

But two personal illustrations relate Billy Graham's popularity as an evangelist in the twentieth century. First, after retiring as a player and later as a college coach at the University of South Carolina, I ran for congress in South Carolina. My first

Ruth Graham, Mrs. Calvin Thielman, Betsy Richardson,
Bobby Richardson, and Dr. Calvin Thielman
(photo courtesy of Bobby Richardson)

check was from Gene Autry and he asked me to come to
California where he owned the California Angels and he'd help
me raise some money for my campaign. He announced at our
Old Timer's game that I was running and that I was conservative. I was honored to have Joe DiMaggio and Mickey Mantle,
both former Yankee greats, to come up and say, "We hear you're
running for Congress. Don't know which ticket but we'll both

fly across the country at our own expense and help in any way."
They both came. Joe came to my hometown in October of
1976. I had just read Chuck Colson's book, *Born Again,* and I
gave him a copy. He wasn't sure at first if he wanted it but after
I said that there'd been a real change in Chuck's life, he took it.

Several weeks later it was reported in *Decision Magazine* that
Joe's brother Vince (there was also Dom who played so well for
the Red Sox) had watched Billy Graham with his wife on television at a crusade. The first night he watched over the sports
page of the paper. The second night he put the paper down.
And the third night watching he got on his knees and accepted Christ and in his words was "born again." I clipped the article out and sent it to Joe.

Only eternity will tell of all that were reached through
God's crusades. But I'd like to close my tribute in an even more
personal way. My wife and I were excited to receive a phone
call from our daughter Christie in the spring of 1998. Her six-
year-old daughter—our granddaughter Anna—had attended a
Billy Graham crusade in Tampa with her dad's youth group. She
was moved to respond to the invitation and she accepted
Christ. What a blessing for Billy's ministry to affect my own
dear family for eternity.

In my own life and ministry there has been one constant: a
loving and caring wife with a servant's heart to stand by and
honor Christ in a way that helped so many, and children that
are following Christ in ministry and their lives. And so Ruth

Graham has been for Billy over the years, influencing many but especially their own. And with Franklin and Ann Lotz and the others, Billy's influence for Christ will indeed continue.

Bobby Richardson joined the New York Yankees at the age of nineteen and they won nine of the next ten American League pennants. After his retirement he coached college baseball at the University of South Carolina. Mr. Richardson also served for ten years as the president of Baseball Chapel.

Dr. Oral Roberts

I am honored and excited to be numbered among the tens of thousands of friends of this number one man of God of our day.

Within my ministry of healing and fulfilling God's call upon my life, Billy has been a friend who at the right moment has said or done the thing that made a major difference in the thoughts of the public leaders toward me. Only he could have done these memorable deeds so lovingly and fearlessly.

His willingness to dedicate Oral Roberts University in April 1967 before eighteen thousand Tulsans and others, all covered by national television, was the incomparable deed that gave ORU life in its infancy.

Billy's totally unashamed stand for the gospel of Jesus Christ, our Savior and Lord, without ever wavering or compromising has been a tremendous encouragement to me to stand tall in my own witness and ministry.

Our personal visits, prayers together, golfing together, and never-failing love for each other are precious.

I believe in Billy Graham, his family, and his worldwide ministry without reservation. Daily I pray for his health. And I

Oral Roberts and Billy Graham
(photo courtesy of Oral Roberts)

never forget we were born in the same year: 1918. (I was born in January and he in November, making him nine or ten months younger.)

Finally, my heart is humbled that God allowed His choice servant to cross my path again and again. God bless my dear and precious friend and brother.

Oral Roberts is the founder of the Oral Roberts Evangelistic Association with its several television programs and the Abundant Life Prayer Group, the University Village retirement complex, and the Oral Roberts University, of which he is chancellor. He has written more than one hundred books including Miracle of Seed Faith.

Dr. M. G. "Pat" Robertson

I was introduced to the Billy Graham ministry when I was a student in college by my mother, who was a devout Christian and a supporter of the handsome young evangelist from North Carolina. My father, who was serving the United States Senate at the time, was one of those on Capitol Hill who lent his support to a man who seemed to be destined to play a major role in the history of evangelical Christianity in the United States. Years later, through my mother's prayers and the grace of the Lord, I accepted Jesus Christ as my personal savior when I was in business in New York City in 1956.

The next year I was a seminary student and volunteered to help in the great Billy Graham crusade at Madison Square Garden that captured the imagination of the financial capital of the world. I will never forget the attendance-setting crowds at Madison Square Garden that summer, and praying with some of those who came forward tearfully at Billy's invitation to accept Jesus Christ as Savior.

Not only did Billy Graham set attendance records at Madison Square Garden, but he packed Times Square for an open-air meeting and did the same things in the shadow of the

Dr. Pat Robertson and Billy Graham
(photo courtesy of Dr. Pat Robertson/CBN)

venerable Federal Reserve Bank in the Wall Street financial district.

Some of us thought that the New York crusade would be the climax of an illustrious life in the service of our Lord. Instead, it was merely the prelude for well over thirty years of unbelievable evangelistic outreach in every continent on the face of the earth.

I cherish the moments that I have spent with Billy—when he has been a guest on my television program, when he was the featured speaker at the opening of our CBN studio headquarters building, when we spent time together at the Brandenburg Gate in Berlin following the collapse of communism, and before that at the Conference for Itinerant Evangelists in Amsterdam.

With all the fame and acclaim that has been heaped upon him, Billy has never wavered in his love of the Lord, in his rock-solid integrity, and in his personal humility. I know of no figure in the evangelical world in the twenty-first century who can approach his stature nor, to the best of my knowledge, has God yet raised up anyone in our country to take his place.

Dr. M. G. "Pat" Robertson is the founder and chairman of the Christian Broadcasting Network, Inc. In 1988 he was a candidate for the presidency and soon after founded the Christian Coalition, with over one million current members. Dr. Robertson has written several books including the bestseller The New World Order.

There was no doubt that at eighteen years of age, God called me to be an evangelist. The communication was as clear as direct conversation: "Evangelist." The definition of what that meant in my young mind was clearly defined by the name, life, and ministry of Billy Graham. At first, he was to me a highly visible and most admirable individual. But within less than thirty-six months, Billy Graham became more than an inspiration; he became a person interested in me. I was a rising young evangelist and someone Dr. Graham believed held promise. He encouraged me by letting me know that he had heard of my effectiveness. Words could never describe what this did in the life of a young man who had grown up without a father. Suddenly the most famous preacher in the world cared about my future and effectiveness.

During brief encounters and treasured moments of communication, Dr. Graham shared with me his concern for his son Franklin, who was attending LeTourneau College in Longview, Texas. I was attending East Texas Baptist College in nearby Marshall. He said, "James, you've got to help win my boy to Christ. He loves to hunt and fish. Take him hunting or fishing . . . do something with him. And share your faith."

Billy Graham and James Robison
(photo courtesy of James Robison)

Several times I communicated with Franklin. We even set a few dates for outdoor experiences, which Franklin canceled. Many years later he told me, "I was probably out drinking beer."

Franklin was truly a rebel in the family and became a subject of our concern and prayers. I remember as though it were yesterday when Dr. Graham shared with me the exciting news of his son's conversion. Billy and T. W. Wilson were in the

Dallas-Fort Worth area tending to precrusade business. They planned a round of golf at Great Southwest Golf Course and asked if I would like to join them. Of course I was thrilled with the opportunity to play. Billy Graham and I rode in a golf cart together. It was a time of relaxation and pure enjoyment. After nine holes, we went to the dining area to have a sandwich.

Billy Graham looked across the table at me with those piercing blue eyes, and within moments they glistened with tears of unspeakable gratitude. Billy commented, "James, did you hear my boy got converted? Franklin gave his life to Christ, and we're so thankful."

T. W. shared personal accounts of how Franklin had confessed Christ and apologized to the family for his years of indifference, rebellion, and selfish pursuits. There was no question in Billy's mind that God had worked a miracle of grace in Franklin's heart.

Years later, Franklin took on a mission—a true mission of mercy. He took over Samaritan's Purse, founded by Bob Pierce. I rejoice in the way God has blessed this wonderful relief and evangelistic outreach. It is also exciting to see Franklin now appointed and in my mind anointed to head up the Billy Graham Evangelistic Association. I had felt this was the wise choice years before the board of directors seemed to willingly recognize and accept it. Praise God!

It is also a thrill to look back and see what God has accomplished and I am so pleased that our own ministry has been able to invest more than a million dollars in the relief efforts of Franklin Graham and Samaritan's Purse.

I want to share why our own ministry is able to be so joyfully involved in serving and assisting others. You see, as I enjoyed God-granted success in crusade evangelism, Billy Graham once again became an instrument of God in my life. I have preached six hundred citywide crusades and spoken to more than fifteen million people. More than 2.5 million individuals have made commitments to Christ at these gatherings. The response has been gratifying—truly supernatural—but there's more to the story . . .

In 1968 I was contacted by PR experts Fred Dienert and Walter Bennett, who had encouraged Billy Graham to begin the radio broadcast known as *The Hour of Decision*. They became close friends to the Graham family. According to Fred and Walter, Billy Graham commented to them while vacationing in Mexico that he did not believe God wanted him to be on a regular television program; his mission was the crusades. He did believe, however, that God had impressed him that a young man named James Robison would be effective in a regular telecast, whether weekly or daily. He really believed God put this on his heart.

Fred and Walter called to ask if I would pray about it. The next week, Fred and his son, Ted, came to visit. I had never considered television because I'm so much a people person and a spontaneous communicator. I thought television was a medium through which I could not effectively utilize the gift God had given me. Billy Graham felt otherwise. So, I took it to the Lord. After five days and nights of seeking God's will, I felt impressed upon that I was to take the gospel message to the masses through television. Once again the communication was conversationally clear. This was God's will.

I stand in amazement at how God has used our television outreach. First, we aired the crusades. As a matter of fact, Billy called after watching a series of crusade messages on prime-time television. He expressed that he had enjoyed them. I asked him if he had any suggestions. He paused a moment and said, "I wish you didn't sweat so much."

Later, we began a weekly interactive program, followed by a daily teaching program. Today we have one of the most widely watched inspirational programs in North America. *LIFE Today* consists of an interactive talk format and airs daily throughout the United States and Canada to more than one hundred million households. We solved the sweating problem by keeping the studio cold. In fact, some of our staff joke about it being a meat locker.

As a result of television, God opened the doors for us to engage in worldwide mission and relief efforts. Remarkably, our missionaries have told us that in Africa alone, the national governments have reported that we have saved more than four million children who would have died without our help. Also, in Africa, more than six million people have made public commitments to Christ as a result of the feeding efforts and the doors opened for crusades. In 2000 alone, more than two million people made commitments to Christ, and similar results have been consistent for the past four years.

We are leading more people to the Lord as a result of television outreach and missions than all the years of crusading combined. So you can see how God used Billy Graham not only to inspire, but also to truly impact multitudes far beyond his own direct and personal ministry.

Billy Graham reached out to encourage one young preacher not once, but several times, and continues to do so to this day. It is with the greatest appreciation that I share these treasured experiences in order to honor a man who truly honors God. Billy Graham is the most gifted communicator of the gospel and a living testimony concerning the power of the gospel's life-changing effect.

Billy, the life of Christ expressed through you in your consistent life of integrity is still your most powerful and effective message. Blessings and gratitude to you and the Graham family.

Since 1962 James Robison has delivered the gospel to the masses— through crusade evangelism and television. He founded LIFE Outreach International to establish effective "Mission Life" outreaches in every population center in the world. Mr. Robison is the author of more than a dozen books including My Father's Place.

Whata an honor and a privilege to be asked to contribute to a book about our wonderful friend Billy Graham.

Billy became a friend of ours (Roy's and mine) during the early days of the Hollywood Christian Group (a group of Christians involved in the entertainment industry). We used to meet monthly to fellowship and had speakers share their testimonies with us. He was such an inspiration to all of us.

During the trip we made to Ireland with Billy, a Dublin priest asked me, "What kind of a man is Billy Graham?"

I replied, "Sir, he is the most consecrated Christian man Roy and I have ever known."

"I knew it," the priest said. "You tell him I said 'God bless his ministry.'"

Billy affects everyone around him in the most positive way. When you meet Billy and see the light that shines from him, you have to believe in God.

Dale Evans Rogers, known as the Queen of the West to her beloved fans, appeared in thirty-five movies with her husband, Roy Rogers. They recorded over four hundred songs together, including their theme

Roy Rogers, Ruth Graham, Billy Graham, and Dale Evans Rogers
(photo courtesy of Dale Evans Rogers)

song, "Happy Trails," which she wrote. Mrs. Rogers penned twenty books and wrote this tribute before her death.

Dabla:During the month of November in the year 2000, I received a small package in the mail from Cliff Barrows, Billy Graham's well-known song leader, board member, and confidant. The parcel contained an audio cassette. It was a copy of the first *Hour of Decision* radio broadcast that originated at the Atlanta Crusade's Ponce de Leon Stadium on November 5, 1950. The cassette was a symbol of fifty years of continuous weekly broadcasting by the evangelist and his team, which in those days consisted of Cliff, Bev Shea, Grady Wilson, Jerry Beaven, and Tedd Smith.

Needless to say, there was much more in the package than an audio tape. There were memories—a host of them.

My relationship with Billy began in 1949 during his Los Angeles crusade in the big tent at Washington and Hill Streets. Late one night after the evening's service, he joined Bob Pierce and drove out to a film editing room in Burbank where I was making *China Challenge,* a motion picture that God would graciously use to summon many to the mission field. As Billy looked over my shoulder at the Moviola screen and saw Bob's footage, which documented appalling needs among Shanghai's boat people, the evangelist caught a vision of how the motion picture could become a tool for evangelism within his own organization.

In a matter of days, Billy Graham Evangelistic Films was born, ultimately becoming known as World Wide Pictures. For fifteen years God gave me the privilege of leading that phase of his ministry from a studio we built next to NBC-Burbank. Dramatic films such as *The Restless Ones, The Heart is a Rebel,* and *Souls in Conflict* accompanied feature documentaries including *Africa on the Bridge, Jerusalem,* and *Decade of Decision.*

Half a century later, Billy's ministry on radio, film, and television continued, augmenting his bestselling books, *Decision Magazine,* a newspaper column and, of course, his platform ministry, which was always at the heart of all that he did through the media.

An incident that stands out in my memory occurred the day I drove him to a major studio to meet producer George Stevens, who was about to direct principal photography on the *Greatest Story Ever Told.* During their conversation, George suddenly became serious and asked, "Dr. Graham, what word of advice can you offer as I start filming the life of Christ?"

After a moment's thought, Billy replied, "Mr. Stevens, treat the miracles as miracles. They were, you know. Don't look for natural causes or explanations. Jesus was God incarnate. 'All power is given unto me in heaven and in earth,' he said to his disciples."

As I listened, it seemed that the Spirit of God was using one to whom had been given the gift of evangelism to guide the making of a motion picture about God's beloved Son ... a film that would be seen by millions around the world.

What has Billy Graham meant to me through the years?

Among so many other admirable qualities, it has been his faithful Christian witness that has given special meaning to our friendship. Whether to individuals in high places who sought his counsel or to the tens of thousands that crowded crusade auditoriums and stadiums around the world, Billy's clear and straightforward presentation of Him who is the Way, the Truth, and the Life challenged me as perhaps none other of God's communicators.

During days of political correctness, when the social climate is one in which those who mention the Name that is above every name are declared to be "insensitive" for fear of offending those of other faiths, Billy Graham has gently but firmly pointed to that One before whom the day will come when every knee shall bow and every tongue confess that Jesus Christ is Lord, to the glory of God the Father (Phil. 2:9-11).

Dick Ross has worked in the communications field for many years in radio, film, and television. He is perhaps best known for his film The Cross and the Switchblade, *starring Pat Boone and Eric Estrada. He served in World War II in the Fifteenth Air Force in Italy, spending part of his time as a prisoner of war in Germany. Mr. Ross currently writes screenplays and books.*

Dr. Robert H. Schuller

I first met Billy Graham when he came as a preacher from
Minnesota to deliver an evangelistic message at the Hope
College Chapel. I sang in the college quartet and we had the
privilege of providing music for him, which meant we were
able to meet him personally, privately, and prayerfully. It was at
that meeting that I first witnessed an altar call. Coming from the
reformed tradition's evangelistic meetings, altar calls were never
in my experience. After all, the strong Calvinist doctrine of
"God's covenant people" did not motivate evangelism as Billy
Graham was delivering it. And so when he offered the altar call,
I didn't rise to my feet, but my heart stepped up and on spiritual legs marched forward with a commitment to Christ that
impacted the rest of my life and made me want to do anything
I could in my ministry to lead persons to make a sincere commitment to Christ as Lord and Savior.

That was in the year 1946. For over half a century, his
books, his ministry have inspired me. In 1969 I was asked to be
the vice chairman of an evangelism committee that would tar-
get bringing Billy Graham to the Angel's Stadium in Anaheim
for a long crusade. I accepted with enthusiasm. One night he

Billy Graham and Dr. Robert H. Schuller
(photo courtesy of Dr. Robert H. Schuller/Crystal Cathedral Ministries)

invited me to "come take a look at the TV truck." He showed
me how they taped the services and would later televise them.
Later that week, while visiting the Crystal Cathedral, he said,
"This church would make a good studio for a weekly televised
church service. Bob, you should think about that. There is no
weekly televised church service on television in Los Angeles—
or in most of America for that matter." When I told him I

didn't believe we could afford it, he said, "Let God make that decision. Let's put out the fleece."

We did. And he and our business administrator prayed for guidance. God delivered. And thanks to Billy we were put on television the first Sunday of November 1970. He launched it. I was simply a part of the program for Christ. It has become the first national televised church service covering America, Russia, and Europe. My ministry would be far less than it is if not for Billy Graham. Truly God's man.

Dr. Robert H. Schuller is pastor of the Crystal Cathedral in Garden Grove, California, home to the weekly Hour of Power *TV church service. His worldwide audience is estimated at ten million persons. Dr. Schuller has authored over thirty books including* Turning Hurts into Halos and Scars into Stars.

Robert H. Straton

In 1950 I left home at the age of seventeen to join the Percy B. Crawford Quartet and went directly to Pinebrook Bible Conference in Stroudsburg, Pennsylvania. When I arrived, I was overwhelmed to learn that George Beverly Shea, Cliff Barrows, and Billy Graham were among the list of speakers and musicians scheduled for a one-day rally during the summer of 1950. We all looked forward to the rally with great anticipation, not only because we were going to sing at the meeting, but because we were hoping to have the opportunity to meet them all personally. That was fifty-one years ago and Billy Graham has been an important figure in my life ever since that day.

Our paths crossed again in April of 1954 at the Harringay Arena in England where Dr. Graham was having a crusade. During that time I was traveling with Percy and Ruth Crawford, and Dr. Graham invited Percy to pray at the meeting and our trio was invited to sing. It was an honor to be with Dr. Graham again and to have the opportunity to sing with Bev Shea and Cliff Barrows.

Walter Bennett and Fred Dienert, two outstanding visionaries, met with Billy Graham in Portland, Oregon, in the spring of 1950 and urged him to go on the ABC network with a weekly one-hour talk-radio program. *The Hour of Decision* was born on November 5, 1950, and Walter Bennett Communications has served as the recording agency for more than fifty years.

For the past thirty-two years I have been a representative of Walter Bennett Communications, and during my tenure I have had the privilege of being with Dr. Graham on many occasions. The most memorable time for me was on one of Billy's visits to Philadelphia. The purpose of his trip was to visit a board member at the University of Pennsylvania Hospital and a foundation on the Main Line. I was given the honor of driving and accompanying Dr. Graham to these appointments, and it was a privilege I will never forget.

Later I was told that it was most unusual for anyone to have that much time alone with Dr. Graham because of his busy schedule. I have always referred to him as Dr. Billy, but when we were in the car he said to me, "Just call me Bill." He is the same gracious gentleman in private that he is when he is on the crusade platform proclaiming the Gospel.

It has been my privilege to serve and assist in the overall outreach of the radio ministry for these many years. *Hour of Decision* is now in its fifty-first year of preaching the Gospel message and the program was honored with the Milestone Award for fifty years of continuous broadcasting at the recent National Religious Broadcasters Convention.

We have counted it a real privilege to represent God's servant and we appreciate the fact that he has remained true to the Word and to his friends these many years.

As a featured soloist with the late Percy B. Crawford's "Youth on the March" program, Robert H. Straton traveled the world singing in some forty countries. He was the founding president of the eastern chapter of the National Religious Broadcasters and presently serves on the board of directors. Mr. Straton is president of Walter Bennett Communications.

Joni Eareckson Tada

It was 1979, the first night of the Budapest, Hungary, Crusade and word raced like wildfire through the stadium that East Germans had slipped through the border and were filling the seats. The wind whipped and clouds threatened, but all of us knew the night was historic. For me, it was historic for another reason: half of the track around the stadium was crowded with disabled people who had come in shabby wheelchairs or were carried on straw mats and on blankets. Before I shared my testimony, tears welled in my eyes when I looked at Dr. Graham and thought, *He preaches to everyone . . . he makes certain the gospel is accessible to everybody!* It's an example I've never forgotten.

Why, I can be sitting up late with college students, haranguing over the meaning of life, or I can be at a dinner party talking to a couple of women in commodities trading, and I think, *What would Mr. Graham say to this group?* You can't give a higher honor to another Christian than to emulate his example. That's why Mr. Graham is a modern-day prophet—convincing and cajoling the rich, the poor, the educated and the illiterate to "come to Him tonight," as he would say. Yes, he's a modern-day prophet because he not only preaches to prime

Billy Graham and Joni Eareckson Tada
(photo courtesy of Joni Eareckson Tada)

ministers and presidents, but to the little, the last, the least, the disenfranchised and forgotten. Even a man carried to a stadium on a piece of ply board.

He reaches everyone. I saw it happen in Budapest.

Joni Eareckson Tada was a teenager when a diving accident left her a quadriplegic. Her story became known around the world through her autobiography, Joni, *and its subsequent full-length feature film. She later founded Joni and Friends, a Christian organization for the disabled community. Mrs. Tada is the author of numerous books including* Holiness in Hidden Places.

Dr. Kenneth Taylor

Billy Graham's influence on other ministries than his own has been incalculable. I give you two examples:

The first has to do with The Living Bible, Paraphrased that might not have been circulated in millions of copies without his influence and recommendation. The first section of The Living Bible was called *Living Letters: The Letters of St. Paul and the Apostles John, James, and Peter.*

Margaret and I used to read these letters from the King James Version to our ten children, but it wasn't easy to keep their attention because of difficult words such as "justification," "righteousness," and "propitiation," and the long sentences.

One day it occurred to me that it might be possible to restate what Paul was saying in a thought-for-thought presentation, saying the same things in current English instead of in the English used four hundred years ago. Then they might find more understanding of the Bible in our family devotional time each evening after supper.

I opened the Bible to the middle of Paul's first letter to Timothy, carefully studied the words of the first verse of the chapter, and then said the same thing in normal English.

Billy Graham and Dr. Kenneth Taylor
(photo courtesy of Dr. Kenneth Taylor/Tyndale House Publishers)

Following this system I went on verse by verse through the chapter, and read it to the children that night. And what I hoped for happened: the children could answer my questions about what Paul said. From time to time I wrote out a chapter in this way, always with good results. Finally I decided to write all the New Testament letters using this method.

I spent the next seven years in my spare time on this project. When it was finally completed, I tried to find a publisher, but no one was interested. So I eventually published two thousand copies myself. These sold slowly until Douglas Judson, personal assistant to Billy Graham and a close friend of mine, took a copy to Billy when he was in a hospital in Hawaii. He was delighted with it and decided to give a free copy to anyone who asked for it when offered to viewers of one of his first televised crusades. The response was overwhelming. The Billy Graham Evangelistic Association had to go back to print again and again, until they had mailed a total of six hundred thousand copies, thus sowing the seed that resulted in Christians and others throughout the nation enjoying the powerful messages of Paul and the others, and flocking to bookstores to purchase additional copies of *Living Letters* for friends.

As each additional section of the Bible was paraphrased— *Living Prophecies, Living Gospels,* etc.—it was used in Billy Graham's television crusades in the same way. And finally, when the entire Living Bible was published in 1972, the Billy Graham Evangelistic Association sent out 1,500,000 copies to the television audience. With this tremendous support and widespread penetration across America, forty million copies of The Living Bible were eventually sold and millions of lives changed to a deeper understanding of God's word and a closer walk with God.

A further development came when Billy insisted, contrary to my desire, that a small royalty be paid on each copy used. Margaret and I set up a foundation to receive all royalties (not only from the Billy Graham Evangelistic Association, but from the other millions of copies distributed through bookstores). As a result many millions of dollars have gone out around the world to mission organizations.

I have only met Billy on two occasions (all the publishing arrangements were made with George Wilson and others in his organization), and I remember those two occasions with deep pleasure.

Something else that has been a blessing to multitudes is The One-Year Bible in its many translations. How did this idea come about? It was reported to me that Billy Graham read something every day from the Old Testament, New Testament, Psalms, and Proverbs. Why not, I thought, publish the Bible in that form, so that these daily readings from every part of the Bible would cover the entire Bible between January 1 and December 31? Billy's idea in this printed form has proved immensely helpful to many, many readers who confess that they had never before read the entire Bible, let alone in one year.

And so I have very much to be thankful to God for in allowing me to be His servant throughout my life. And thanks to Billy Graham for his part in giving me opportunities for serving God in the ways I have just described.

Dr. Kenneth Taylor's concern for his children's confusion over the meaning of the King James text inspired him to write Living Letters. *This was followed by the complete* The Living Bible, *published in 1971 with over forty million copies sold. Dr. Taylor is chairman of the board of Tyndale House Publishers.*

I n 1978 Reverend Dr. Billy Graham organized a crusade at the Singapore National Stadium. Although I was not interested I reluctantly relented to my wife's unstoppable persuasion.

The drive to the crusade was an ordeal. The roads were jam-packed but we eventually arrived at the stadium . . . with a loud bang. I soon realized that my car had just exploded from overheating. As we continued to chug along it came to a complete stop in a parking lot.

Earlier I had wanted to turn around. However, as my car was totally immobilized, I had no choice but to attend the crusade even though I was fuming mad inside.

The stadium was overflowing and the singing had already stopped. Billy Graham spoke, but as we had the worst seats imaginable we heard nothing except his altar call. I was moved to respond as I felt a deep sense of peace in me and I felt the presence of God. All I wanted to do was to say, "Thank you, God, whoever you are."

Soon someone came to fill out a form with me. I would not normally respond to a stranger who wanted my personal particulars but I recognized the name on the tag. Unbeknownst to

Professor Khoo Oon Teik, who attended to me, I was someone he had spoken to a few days earlier regarding some business needs. I thought he attended to me because he knew who I was.

When the meeting ended we went back to our car not expecting to drive home. But when the ignition was turned on I was astonished that the car started and we drove home without incident.

The next day Professor Khoo invited me to join his Bible study group and eventually that group moved to my home and since then we have been meeting for the last twenty-two years.

I have always wondered if it is possible for so many coincidences to occur in one night. With hindsight I am convinced that it was God's divine plan for me.

I had my share of challenges. A year after I accepted Jesus as Savior I discovered that our eldest son, who was ten years old, was suffering from *retinitis pigmentosa,* an incurable eye condition that leads to total blindness. Instead of wallowing in self-pity we committed his visual impairment to God. With God's grace and an unyielding spirit, our son wrestled to overcome his disability with courage and fortitude. He will soon complete his Ph.D. dissertation at Cambridge University in England. My second son, who recently graduated from Yale, and my daughter, a freshman at Yale, have also accepted Jesus as Lord.

My life is evidence that God will not permit any troubles to come upon me unless He has a specific plan by which great blessing can come out of the difficulty. However I must remain united with Jesus Christ all the time. Only when I do will I be able to live a victorious life beyond hope. Thank you, Billy, for introducing my family and me to our Lord Jesus.

Dr. Yip Yan Wong is the founder of the East Asian Wywy Group, an agglomeration of companies dealing in such markets as direct sales, distribution, financial services, marketing, and real estate, among others. Among numerous other posts, Dr. Wong holds the inaugural chair of the Singapore Committee of the Pacific Basin Economic Council representing one thousand companies with a combined revenue of four trillion dollars.

Louis Zamperini

As a youngster, I was poisoned against religious tent meetings on the outskirts of my hometown. It sent chills up my spine as I lifted the side of the tent to get a peek at a screaming evangelist and a boisterous congregation that seemed out of control. It was frightening to a young boy. This frightful image stuck with me throughout my life.

However, in 1949 I did attend a tent gathering in Los Angeles. With the childhood image of a tent meeting still vivid in my mind, any chance of a spiritual experience for me would be extremely remote, if not impossible.

My wife, Cynthia (the persuader), and I entered a huge tent at Washington and Hill Streets in Los Angeles. My attitude about such places had not changed until I stepped inside. I found a throng of people, much to my surprise and relief, under control. I got my second surprise when a fellow named Billy Graham was introduced. My mental picture of an evangelist also changed as this tall, handsome, clean-cut, athletic type walked to the podium.

Billy held his Bible open in his left hand and thus began his message. The entire focus of his sermon was on Jesus Christ, the

Son of God. His was the only name under heaven whereby we could be saved, Billy would say. Then he would exclaim, "I didn't say that. God said it here in the Scriptures." I was impressed. Here was a man speaking with true sincerity and deep conviction—honestly and totally committed to God.

The following day, when Billy gave the invitation, I gave my life to Christ and found that salvation through Christ Jesus was real. My spiritual compass turned from south to north. I began a new life in Christ.

Since my conversion, like so many others, I have watched Billy's life and ministry. These are my conclusions drawn fifty-plus years later:

First, he has never compromised the preaching of the gospel or wavered from the truth.

Second, he has never retaliated against those who have ridiculed him.

Third, he has maintained a full set of armor against the fiery darts of the enemy.

Fourth, though closely scrutinized, he has never been involved in a compromising situation.

Fifth, he is a man of sacrifice and unhesitating service to God.

Sixth, humility has been his God-given trademark.

Seventh, as a loving father and a godly husband, he has motivated the Graham family children to have the same vigorous devotion to Christ as their father and mother have demonstrated.

Eighth, because of his Christlike values and commitment to the Great Commission, he has been honored by royalty and world leaders and yet he ministers to the masses and down-and-outers with compassion.

Ninth, the expanse of his ministry has no equal and only God knows of the scores of changed lives. The infrastructure of crime throughout the world has been reduced by the renewal of countless erring souls.

Tenth, Billy is truly a gold-medal winner and I am a better Christian because of his walk.

Louis Zamperini held the world's interscholastic mile record for twenty years. He was the first American to finish the 5,000-meter in the 1936 Berlin Olympics. He also served as a captain in the U.S. Air Force during World War II, spending two and a half years as a prisoner of Japan. Captain Zamperini's life was featured by CBS in a documentary aired during the closing ceremonies of the 1998 Nagano Winter Olympics.

D. Billy Graham has been a hero of mine for many years. I have never met him personally, but have seen him on television often and have been greatly influenced by his life's example. I don't recall which of these two following events took place first, but I do know the impact of each was great and undoubtedly protected me from grief and heartache.

Not long after I was saved on July 4, 1972, I heard Dr. Richard Peacock, minister to adults at First Baptist Church, Dallas, utter a beautiful prayer. A young girl had been kidnapped and Dr. Peacock was praying that God would build a wall of fire around her and protect her from harm. He asked God to return her just as she was when she was taken. When I heard that prayer, chill bumps ran all over me. At that moment I asked God to build a wall of fire around me and protect me from temptation. I promised God that if He would do that so that I would not have to use my energy to fight temptation, I would use my energy to serve Him. To be candid, I do not know if that event took place first, or if I had already committed to follow Dr. Graham's example.

I do know this: I have not been seriously tempted sexually,

financially, or morally since the day I prayed that prayer. However, I must confess that I have been extraordinarily careful. Here's where Dr. Graham's influence comes in, and to the best of my ability I have followed his example. This process has worked for me and I am deeply grateful that Dr. Graham has set such a high standard and has been a marvelous role model for me and millions of other men and women all over the world. He truly is God's man for this critical time in our country and world's history. He honors God in word and deed and gives God the glory for letting him be a servant to and for a sinful world. Like Dr. Graham, my perfect role model is Christ, so I regularly ask, "Does it glorify God?" and largely make my decisions on the answer to that question. I believe that's what Dr. Graham does.

Zig Ziglar is an author and speaker whose books, tapes, videos, and printed training tools have remained at the top of media sales. A well-known authority on the science of human potential, Mr. Ziglar has been recognized three times in the Congressional Record of the United States for his achievements. He is the author of numerous books including Over the Top.